Gorky, Russia;
First man in

Gorky, Russia; First man in

Memoirs from being the first American allowed
inside Russia's closed exile city

DONN G. ZIEBELL PH.D.

**The KGB and Moscow's Ministry of Education
approved a U.S. business seminar series**

Front Cover Image Creation by Ben Gustafson; Vibrenti
Author's photograph by Ben Gustafson; Vibrenti

ISBN-10: 0989474534
EAN-13: 9780989474535

Also by this Author

**My Letters to a Prisoner –
I had not met**

Author's true life experiences written to a
man serving a seven year prison sentence

Conceal Carry; Pause

The Pursuit of Trained Readiness and
a Discipline for Self-Defense Survival

To my seven grandchildren,

Lauren Emily (Baker) Fischer
David Michael Baker
Brittney Jean Ziebell
Joel Harrison Baker
Benjamin Quinn Gustafson
Kenyan Corinne Gustafson
Sky DaShaun Gustafson

In anticipation that your careers will
provide security, timely rewards,
with enjoyable experiences to
exceedingly fill your lives.

Acknowledgement

I am grateful for Dolores "Dee" Oyler's many hours of editing and helping make the manuscript chapters well-worded for exceptional reading enjoyment and for assistance from my daughter, Jody Gustafson, for providing final proof editing to ensure we reach our goal of excellence.

I especially thank Robert D. Shuster, Archivist, and Katherine J. Graber, Public Services Archivist, for retrieving and assisting with my Slavic Gospel Association personal files, interviews and notebooks archived in the Billy Graham Center at Wheaton College.

Foreword

It is not unusual to question ourselves and think about our life accomplishments that we value. Then we might happen upon information about someone like Picasso, who is reported to have created one painting a day; his output was astounding!

13,500 paintings
100,000 graphic prints or engravings
34,000 book illustrations
300 sculptures and ceramics [1]

This should not discourage us from achieving any kind of personal goal. By chance, something can come along to challenge us into action; for instance, I happened upon an author's Internet presentation. One thing he said impressed me: "If you already have created a body of research in the past, then why stall? Use it for writing."

I realized I had a body of recorded life experiences that qualified as material for a book. It contained a record of the most unusual, fascinating, cross-cultural adventure in my life. It took over a year to write and

---

1 PicassoMio, *picassomio.com/art-articles/picasso-how-many-artworks-did-picasso-create-in-his-lifetime,* (accessed August 16, 2015)

self-publish. I believe it will give many people a surprising amount of reading enjoyment: *Gorky, Russia; First man in.*

I agree with people that believe in the motto: "Books change Lives." It is my hope that in some way this book will add a change in your life.

"Секрет бытия человека не только жить
но есть ради чего жить"

Федор Достоевский

*"The secret of a man's being is not only to live
but to have something worthy to live for. "*

FYODOR DOSTOYEVSKY

Preface

After just completing a successful five-year run with my own manufacturing consulting firm, I hit the wall during the 1985 U.S. business slump. At the time I was waiting for approval of four contracts worth $4.2 million to install robots in a huge manufacturing plant. Plant engineers promised that at least two of the contracts would be approved. It turned out to be untrue. My wife said, "Donn, there is no money coming in!"

I received a notice of a job opening. I called and learned the Executive Vice President position was still open. The Board of Directors had recently created this new position.

During the interview the president said, "Donn, two vice presidents and I are black-listed by the KGB. We cannot enter Russia. Join our organization, and maintain your annual State registration for your S Corporation." That was strange but I did not sense I would be at any risk.

After working many years for manufacturing corporations, I never would have imagined the different path my career would take. Was I really the first American to enter Gorky, Russia? My encounters and experiences will hold your interest.

Contents

Part I

U.S. BUSINESS EXPERIENCE

People might view my job changes like a train wreck. Upon looking back I consider it a priceless learning experience controlled by a divine hand with a plan.

Faithless is he that says farewell
when the road darkens

J. R. R. TOLKIEN

One

UNEXPECTED CAREER CHANGES

In one initial job interview late in my career I was told to keep my consulting firm alive. The president then said, "Three of us are blacklisted by the KGB. We cannot get into Russia." I had no idea where to "file" this odd comment or if it would ever impact my life; but one day it did.

But I must start at the beginning, 28 years before the above experience. I graduated in 1957 with a B.S. degree in Metallurgical Engineering. This degree, I believed, would be an asset, since it could open the door to employment in multiple types of manufacturing industries. It was a career title that most laymen could not pronounce, spell or understand. Once, when I told a man I had graduated from Missouri School of Mines & Metallurgy, he asked, "Are you a psychiatrist?"

I became unemployed twice during my first four years in industry, 1957 to 1961. Each time, my wife witnessed my return home with a car load of my technical books. A 2015 article in TIME magazine speaks on current (2015) U.S. employment.[1]

---

1 Anne Kreamer, "Why it's risky to be risk-averse," TIME magazine, June 22, 2015, 33.

- "According to the Bureau of Labor statistics, people now in their 50s have on average held a half-dozen jobs since they were 25. For Gen X-errs and millennials, the average is surely higher and rising - - -
- The writer continued: "I discovered that more than half of all Americans at all levels of the workforce are thinking of changing not only their jobs but also their careers. But of those who want to change, roughly 50% have no clue on how to figure out the next chapter.
- "In this new world, having a single Hail Mary Plan B is no longer enough. We need to tee up Plan Cs, again and again and again, throughout our working lives."

Kaiser Aluminum

My first layoff was due to a corporate policy unknown to me until I was escorted out the door. The Kaiser Aluminum extrusion plant in Halethorpe, Maryland, was closing on my three-year anniversary with them. At the time, my wife and I had two young children, and she and I had just become Christians. We decided to remain in Catonsville, where we were beginning to experience spiritual growth. It didn't seem right to walk away from the church where we were growing in our faith.

I truly believe my decision to remain with our church and not relocate resulted in God's continuous provision of spiritually blessing our marriage and family. In addition, the Southern state Kaiser selected for my transfer was known for having a poor educational system. After my decision to stay put, I immediately began to search for other industrial employment options in Baltimore, as I continued solving metallurgical problems with follow-up by writing technical reports.

To buy time, I asked to be considered for a transfer to any one of Kaiser's other aluminum plants. However, as I left the office of the

Director of the Technical Department, he made a quick, unspoken decision about my request. Sixty minutes later I was escorted out the factory door to the parking lot by my supervisor, who became Kaiser Aluminum Corporate President a number of years later. Standing by my car in the parking lot, I realized a request for a different transfer destination was never an option. Apparently, there was a corporate policy that any job transfer offer not accepted resulted in the immediate termination of an employee. It also meant no severance pay.

Gibson & Kirk Foundry

Within three weeks I was hired by G&K Foundry in Baltimore to monitor their metal melting process change-over from gas-fired to electric melting furnaces. This change caused a crisis for some foundries as they lost control over alloy chemistry. G&K was successful; the metallurgy of all our different metal alloys continued to meet industrial specifications. With the firm's feared technical risk now over, I no longer was needed and was gracefully terminated in 1961 with four weeks of severance pay after exactly one year of employment.

The good news was I was able to reopen a job offer from Martin-Marietta that I had turned down when I joined G&K Foundry. During my twelve months with G&K, my year-old previous offer had increased with a generous growth in starting salary. It well exceeded what I would have been earning if I had accepted their offer a year earlier.

Martin-Marietta Nuclear Division

I accepted Martin-Marietta's new offer and immediately began working in their Nuclear Division. I developed the metallurgical processes for the manufacture of stainless steel-clad, enriched fissionable uranium U^{235} nuclear fuel elements for a customer's newly-designed super heater for an atomic power reactor, a first of its kind. The windowless cement walls

5

within which I worked stopped the enriched uranium radiation from escaping to the outside environment. We wore a small clip-on dosage meter to measure the cumulative U^{235} radiation dosage our bodies received while working in the restricted manufacturing areas.

By1966, my fifth year in the nuclear industry, a nationwide fear of nuclear power plants began to develop. As I continued to work on manufacturing reactor fuel elements, environmentalist groups ignited a national concern that caused a public ground swell against nuclear power plants. There had been no U.S. nuclear power plant accidents up to this time, yet Martin-Marietta was not receiving new requests for price quotations for future production orders to manufacture fuel elements.

Martin-Marietta redirected their focus toward radioactive isotopes for heat generation joined with thermoelectric elements to generate electric power within satellites. I sensed a possible threat against my employment, so early in 1966 I informed my university I was job searching.

Two

SUCCESSFUL PERFORMANCE NETS JOB LOSS

Huyck Metals Company

A fiber metal products company on the East Coast scouted for a Metallurgical Engineer. After contacting my university, Huyck Metals Company in Milford, Connecticut, called, interviewed and hired me in 1966.

Huyck supplied manufactured fiber metal materials used to improve performance in the air compressor section in jet engines. Their customers were all world class major jet engine manufacturers. Huyck's fiber metal technology was a money-maker "protected" under a U.S. Troy Patent. Their major competitor, Brunswick Corporation, was suspected of infringing on the Troy Patent license with their own fiber metal products.

Within Huyck it was strongly believed no one could prove Brunswick's patent infringement. I had an idea for a way to test the competitor's product and was given the green light to proceed. Fortunately, my laboratory test results proved without a doubt Brunswick infringed on our Patent. Our lawyers sued Brunswick.

Having greater financial resources, Brunswick was smart and responded strategically. They purchased Huyck Metals, rather than fight a lawsuit. Brunswick's purchase negotiations required Huyck's management to reduce 40% of overhead costs before their plant takeover. I was among the third group of terminated employees.

Schick Safety Razor Divison

It was 1972, a time of a national business slump in the engineering job market. It took several months for me to get even one interview that might produce a job offer. I was hired and remained employed for three years as Blade Finishing production superintendent in the Schick Safety Razor plant of Warner-Lambert Corporation. During this employment, I completed a MBA degree by taking night school classes at the University of New Haven.

Brunswick Corporation

I was surprised by a call from the Corporate V.P. of Manufacturing over Brunswick's Technical Products Divisions and the Plant Manager of Brunswick Fiber Metals Division, (formerly Huyck Metals), asking me to meet with them. They wanted me back to be their Manager of Manufacturing. I gladly accepted their offer.

Unknown to me, the current Plant Manager was to be promoted to Director of Manufacturing for the Technical Products Division in twelve months. After forty years with Brunswick, he was transferred to corporate headquarters in Skokie, Illinois, where he eventually retired. So, within one year, I was promoted to Plant Manager as his replacement.

Twelve months later the hammer fell. I was directed to put the plant's production output into extra high gear, maintain the supply of fiber metal products to five jet engine companies and, at the same time, build an extra twelve-month supply of inventory. My plant and two other Brunswick plants were scheduled to be moved and consolidated into Brunswick's large Deland, Florida, plant.

As I accomplished production acceleration, I knew this consolidation meant Brunswick would have three chiefs for every management position, i.e., three Plant Managers, three Quality Control Managers, three Engineering Managers, etc. I could not get any commitment about the position they planned for me – if any. I decided it was time to consider a career move.

Despite my earlier layoffs, overall U.S. manufacturing employment opportunities were good. Every job change I made or was forced to make provided advancement in position and salary. Before informing Brunswick about my decision to leave, I interviewed and received an immediate offer. I managed the Brunswick plant to its closing and announced I had secured a position with another corporation. Brunswick honored me with a departing banquet and a gift of a fine Bulova Accutron wristwatch, the best I ever had. It was engraved, "Thanks from Brunswick."

Talley Industries

I became the Assistant Director of Corporate Manufacturing for Talley Industries. I was able to continue living in Connecticut and travel to subsidiary plants within Talley. This included special assignments in clock plants, plastic molding operations, and many other product plants, including one plant making military jet pilot ejection seats designed to save the lives of pilots.

My achievements were noticed. I was promoted in 1979 to be the National Director of Customer Service that handled consumer complaints for products made by both Seth Thomas and Westclox clock plants. They moved my family 1,000 miles to Illinois, close to where my wife and I had lived and attended high school together. It was only the second household move I had to make in my entire career. Two of our kids were in eastern colleges at the time, and our youngest child was in seventh grade.

Talley Corporate directive to me for my new position was threefold:

1.) Bring the cost of National Customer Service under control.
2.) Improve customer service and satisfaction on product complaints from customers.
3.) Succeed in satisfying customers so they stop writing to the Board of Directors with their complaints about poor Customer Service.

I was given four years to achieve these objectives, but I accomplished them in two years. The editors of **Good Housekeeping** magazine told their readers that Westclox had improved their handling of customer product complaints. They printed this acknowledgement in their September, 1981 issue. [1]

During January 1981, while I was focusing my attention on maintaining our good Customer Service performance, Talley Industries fell out of the Fortune 500 list. I was aware of the strong office politics existing inside the headquarters of the two clock subsidiaries I supported with National Customer Service. Whether good or bad, I was 1,000 miles away from both clock manufacturing divisions. Talley Corporation's decision to consolidate both clock subsidiaries and National Customer Service into the Athens, Georgia, plant was unknown to me at that time.

The VP of Manufacturing from the Westclox Athens plant flew up to my National Service Center for a visit. He spent two days looking around

1 Charlotte Montgomery, "HAIL!," *Good Housekeeping*, September 1981, 24.

and briefly meeting with me to get acquainted with our process and performance for handling U.S. consumer product complaints.

Unknown to me, the VP's agenda contained a hidden directive. He asked me to drive him to the airport. Upon pulling up to the United terminal, he grabbed his bag, stepped out of my car, turned and said, "You need to know you are being terminated!" and hurriedly walked away.

That I was stunned is an understatement! What a classic example of bad managerial practice!

I called Talley's Corporate Treasurer in Phoenix who had originally approved my hiring by Talley and was the officer who had transferred me to my present position. He said he was sorry and affirmed my termination, saying the decision had been made by the southern Athens plant president. He asked how much time I needed, and I was granted my 30-day request.

When I arrived home the fourth time with my carload of books, my wife asked, "Now what are you going to do?" I answered, "Become a manufacturing consultant," then explained what I hoped this would become. It was still five years before the unusual interview comment mentioned at the beginning of Chapter 1 would occur. So, in 1981, I launched my consulting firm. A mix of both unexpected fortune and misfortune would follow.

Three

The interview that included mentioning the KGB was still five years in the future. My consulting firm was established in 1981. It was located in the English basement of my home with above-ground windows that provided daylight and a view of the yard and woods. A used desk and chair, two new double drawer horizontal file cabinets and a telephone were all that furnished the "headquarters" of Ziebell Associates, Inc. Checking and savings accounts were opened with $5,000 of capitalization used to register corporate legal documents for Illinois Incorporation.

Ziebell Associates Inc.

One word describes starting a consulting practice from ground zero: difficult. There wasn't any type of industry that was excluded from my marketing effort. I began as one man working alone and exploring all kinds of possibilities. One high-volume manufacturer of deep drawn aluminum cans wanted to further increase production efficiency. After viewing their operation, I wrote the best possible targeted proposal for them to consider. They never acted upon it.

I was able to gain a two-week consulting assignment to evaluate the manufacturing personnel, inter-relationships and production efficiency in a potato chip plant in Louisville, Kentucky. Then a friend who did marketing promotion for a small Chicago company mentioned my availability as a consultant. The owner hired me for a month-long study of his small company that was beset with some internal dysfunction. Both this contract and the Louisville contract culminated with reports to top managements detailing my findings. The reports were very-well-received and opened their eyes to some of my findings. Both small contracts helped build my self-confidence and provided a consulting start-up track record. But anyone who "cold calls" on companies must have a thick skin to accept being turned away without an opportunity to meet or speak with a key company executive.

World Renowned Consultant

Information I gathered from researching the Thomas Register and publications containing factual information about firms was helpful preparation. I learned executives' names, as well as product information for cold-calling different sized manufacturing companies. But I seldom got beyond the receptionist. On one occasion, I called a Chicago consultant who worked solo. Donald R. Booz was one of the most well-known names in the history of the consulting world. He had an office in the Chicago Lyric Opera House. To my surprise, he responded to my recorded telephone message, which had been a "shot-in-the-dark" attempt to reach him.

He invited me to the surprisingly small office he shared with his secretary. I concluded it was his post-retirement consulting practice. Learning how he was working on a networking principle was very helpful. He had other independent consultants with distinct specialties upon whom he called when a specialization outside his consulting discipline was required. He expressed interest in me as a manufacturing consultant. The manufacturing person working with him had been hired full time by a large consulting firm and was no longer available to him.

So the deal was that, if he had something that came up in the manufacturing area, he would call me to act as his specialist in manufacturing. Likewise, he told me that if I ever landed an opportunity that required human resource and personnel issues to be resolved, he would give me one half day of his time. He said, "My chauffeur will drive me to any destination in the greater Chicago region." He would help me secure a contract portion that dealt with his expertise, while I would work to secure the manufacturing portion. I left his office elated with this tentative relationship.

Meeting with him taught me how to expand the capability of Ziebell Associates, Inc. by establishing independent consulting agreements with other specialists in order to have a broader appeal to corporations needing consulting services. I proceeded to make legal associate status agreements with a product packaging expert, an electrical and process controls engineer, a mechanical engineer who managed his own mechanical design and equipment fabrication shop, a sales marketing businessman, and a theoretician able to handle process analysis using mathematical analysis for unstructured problem-solving. The Chicago human resources and personnel consultant, Donald R. Booz, also was available. Now Ziebell Associate's marketing brochure gave credibility as to having more manufacturing disciplines that could be put to work on any consulting contract.

Beatrice Foods

Beatrice Foods called me in; I was accompanied by three Ziebell Associates. They hired us to observe and study a snack foods plant in Ohio. (The aversion I already had to that snack food was reinforced after seeing the main ingredient was the skin of pigs). Their directive was: report your findings and present them in a meeting. Their plant used a pretty efficient multi-step batch process. Our measurements on the process steps found a bit more efficiency was possible. Their oven cooking process step was restricting daily production output. We presented our findings with the mathematical analysis to support our solution for increasing daily output with customized automated control systems. We received no response but soon learned the Beatrice Corporation had been bought out.

Keebler Company

Ultimately, the marketing approach that did work was persistence. I made three cold call visits to the corporate headquarters of a well-known national cookie company with many plants around the US. Each time I called, the receptionist for the Vice President of Manufacturing delivered his message, "Tell Mr. Ziebell I cannot see him at this time." Fortunately, he had my business card.

A few weeks later on a Monday, this vice president called and asked me to come to his office the next day. When he received me, he said my persistence had paid off. He revealed he had two manufacturing problems. "One is a personnel problem that I cannot tell you about." Then for the second problem he said, "I have a manufacturing vision which everyone in our company as well as experts in the food machinery industry say cannot be done." He added, "I am unable and not permitted to tell you any of the details or specifics."

He continued, "Please, write a proposal detailing how you might solve these two problems and have it in my hands by Thursday morning (two days away) for an important meeting I am attending that afternoon." I left excited and determined I would do what he asked. My proposal was short, to the point and used an approach that was the best I could do without any insight into the problems. Attached to my Manufacturing Consultants marketing brochures was this single page proposal that essentially said the following:

1.) For your personnel problem, I will bring in a world-renowned personnel consultant, whose name you immediately will recognize.
2.) For your manufacturing problems, my team of experts will study your product and the manufacturing process, learn both in detail from A-Z, conceptualize and arrive at an innovative machine design solution and prove it by physically creating a process to demonstrate it can be accomplished.

I heard nothing for two weeks. Then the Vice President of Manufacturing called and invited me to meet with his Vice President of Engineering to discuss the manufacturing problem. However, he no longer needed to address the personnel problem, because it had been resolved right after he requested my proposal. "Shucks!" Unfortunately, that meant I would not have the memorable opportunity to introduce the world-renowned consultant to him.

I was introduced to the V. P. of Engineering. As he talked, I grasped the fact that he was energized and wanting to move forward on solving the manufacturing problem. He expressed his desire to use Ziebell Associates, Inc. for their manufacturing problem-solving project. Unknown to me at that time, this project would add up to $979, 000 over the three-year contract that included three phases to the project as follows:

Contract Phase I: Visit their bakery in Michigan and study their product and production process to understand the challenge in solving a baking industry's "Pandora's box." After they received our report, they said something unusual: "You have learned more about our product than we knew."

Contract Phase II: Conceptualize how the problem would be solved. Our conceptualization was submitted in three weeks. The client said they did not receive their money's worth. Naturally, this phase contained nothing to visually see, only our conceptualization in ethereal words! But in further conversation, they did agree that it was a brain effort of creative conceptualization for our problem-solving exercise to decide what specific details had to be accomplished by inventing the process. Upon agreeing with us, they said they wanted us to go forward with the project. Next we had to present to them a project proposal and cost estimate for Phase III.

Contract Phase III: Proposal: design, build a pilot line and install it in their Atlanta, Georgia, bakery to prove that it works on one row of 120-per-minute baked cookies coming out of a continuously-running baking oven. We could not tell them what we were going to invent and build until we invented it. But they approved this major phase of the contract, because they knew we understood their product and ultimate goal very well. We moved forward to prove our creative problem-solving ability as a manufacturing consulting firm.

When the Phase III contract was signed, our work began immediately. My son Tory had just graduated from New England College. The job offers he had received lacked good opportunities for potential career growth, so he came to Illinois and joined the two key engineering associates involved in this huge contract. His role was yet to be defined.

Four

Computer Suggested

Mark, our Electrical Controls Engineer, came into my office at the beginning of the contract's Phase III. "Donn, if we want to be a real consulting firm, we need a computer." It was 1982 when computers were touted as being the future best thing. I agreed and asked my son Tory to go out and shop for a computer. He said he did not know a thing about computers. I told him to start visiting computer stores and learn from talking to computer sales people.

He quickly gained knowledge from different computer salesmen. In fact, he thought he might even know more than the average sales person. So he selected a computer for us. It seems like a wild expenditure now forty years later; but in 1982, we paid $10,000 for an IBM floppy disc computer including a massive dot matrix printer. We used it for proposal and report writing, tracking our design progress, purchase orders and recording expenditures. Jim, our accountant, used it for payables, payroll checks, and financial accounting.

Manpower & Progress

Two major activities took most of the first year of this three-year contract: 1) Ken, as mechanical design engineer, was inventing many machines that had to be fabricated and assembled into one continuous processing line to package irregular shaped, home-baked-style cookies; and 2.) Mark had to design all the electrical motion controls, electrical integration of all the machines with programmable controls and an operator control panel. He had to figure out how to weigh every cookie speeding by at a speed of 120 cookies per minute, record their weight and direct each cookie to one of two alternative destinations to optimize packaging within the tolerance of final bag weight specifications.

My firm was renting office and shop space from Ken and paying him to employ his designers, machine fabricators and electricians. The size of this contract utilized all of his shop space and manpower of six employees. Ken was a gifted engineer, but on occasions he and I got into a twit with one another. He admitted he was manic depressive, which explained why I often felt I was on an emotional roller coaster when we met to iron out problems.

Tory played a key role in smoothing out communications within the team, and he kept tabs on the progress of the machine assembly. Ken's personality and emotional cycles partly added to our project running eight months beyond the intended contract delivery deadline. However, Mark's electrical process control design was pushing the state-of-art, so the delay was a help to him. Thankfully, he was our "Steady Eddy" who made all the machines become one extraordinary integrated system with every machine action working together like a symphony.

Our client faithfully maintained scheduled monthly payments. Because we were behind schedule, at one point I had $250,000 of our client's cash in my corporate savings account. A person could go wild sitting on so much cash. I had to exercise extreme control, since I had a moral obligation to complete the project within budget. The client was informed we were behind schedule, so they visited us to understand and learn where our progress stood. When they saw our invention of shiny stainless steel machines and our electrical process controls, as well as our effective handling of the stream of speeding, individually-weighed cookies, they left believing in us. Our delivery delay was understood, because we were accomplishing what the entire cookie industry said could not be done!

"Gold" Estimate

There was great optimism within Ziebell Associates. Our million-dollar machine gave an expectation for potential great personal wealth. Why? Cookies come out of a baking oven delivering 120 cookies a minute per row multiplied by sixteen rows wide, equaling 1,920 cookies per minute. Our pilot line was handling only <u>one</u> row of cookies. Cookie bakeries can have four or more baking ovens running twenty four hours a day. Our client had many cookie bakeries around the country. The multiplying factors meant that our successful cookie machine could conceivably result in Ziebell Associates becoming a multi-million dollar cookie equipment manufacturer for our client. This meant the possibility of significant wealth.

Atlanta Bakery

Ken got into one of his twits as the project was coming to an end. The pilot line was disassembled, strapped onto wooden shipping skids ready for an equipment rigger to transport it by truck for delivery to the Atlanta bakery, where installation and testing would take place. This would be the ultimate proof we had achieved the goal for which the client contracted us. Ken unexpectedly announced he was not going to travel to

Atlanta. Fortunately, Hank, Ken's shop foreman, said he would go with us. Hank saved the day, since he knew in detail every machine Ken had designed, as well as all the integrated electrical system that Mark had designed. Hank had assembled the entire pilot line once in Illinois. Mark, Hank, Tory and I went to Atlanta for the installation into the Atlanta bakery.

Successful Pilot Line

Our invention was received with some awe as it worked and accomplished packing irregular shaped "home baked" cookies into bags within the industry weight specifications. Furthermore, it packed within an even tighter weight range than industry specifications required and resulted in additional economic savings benefit from tighter optimized cookie package weights.

Yet, we sensed the bakery floor supervisors gave evidence of dissatisfaction. Each baking oven employed 30 hourly women hand packaging cookies, multiplied by three shifts around the clock, then multiplied by four baking ovens in the plant. Our invention had the economic benefit of eliminating 360 low skill workers' jobs from the plant payroll. Assume they made $8.50 an hour in 1985. The plant would save $6 million per year in labor savings and make the plant profit increase by that amount.

The tragedy for Atlanta was that these mostly minority workers would lose their livelihood. This was a good example of automation playing havoc with the lives of hourly workers. Certainly God had a solution to this very bad situation, and it soon would be revealed.

Five

An Uncertain Destiny

The outlook for huge dollar contracts for cookie packaging systems caused our hopeful anticipation. But the destiny of manufacturing and selling of any kind of products in the marketplace is driven by marketing people. Two weeks after the success of the pilot line, our client's marketing department fired a shot that killed the bright future of Ziebell Associates.

Earlier in 1985, our client had heard about one of their competitor's plans to launch a new product called "soft batch cookies." Soft batch cookies lacked the firmness necessary to be handled by automated machines and had to be hand packed. Our client's marketing department hired a Chicago promotional marketing firm to help them become the first cookie company to promote and deliver soft batch cookies to market. This was the death blow to our technology breakthrough for machine packaging of home-baked cookies. Closing out the contract allowed me to distribute $16,000 completion bonus checks to Mark, Ken and myself.

Tory knew that my business was hitting the wall without a future with the cookie-packaging invention, which was owned by Keebler. He decided to return to New Hampshire, find a job and live there. My other associates were no longer active in my business, except Mark, who remained after the cookie machine contract ended.

Zenith Company

Months before we were to deliver the pilot line to Atlanta, I had expanded my consulting marketing effort. One result was that I was able to meet engineers at Zenith's TV vacuum picture tube plant. They were interested in exploring the possibility of installing robots in certain places along their production line to improve productivity and reduce labor costs. I was taken into their glass vacuum tube assembly line to watch how a worker would put a black aqua-dag coating, having electrical properties, onto an applicator, then manually reach inside the narrow neck of a vacuum tube and coat the neck with a 360^0 swirl of the hand. They did not believe this human hand movement inside the narrow necks could be automated.

Fortunately for us, Mark and I had previously visited two different nearby robot companies. We talked to their engineers about their robots' capabilities, and they had allowed us some hands-on experience exercising the dexterity of their robots for manufacturing applications. We had a very good grasp how far the robots could extend their reach, and we learned the limits of dexterity and the maximum horizontal rotational travel reach within a work station.

Next Mark and I were escorted by a Zenith engineer to observe four glass vacuum tube assembly line stations to see the exact applications for which they would like to consider robots.

Mark and I believed robots could perform all four operations. Within a week Zenith signed a $14,000 contract for us to first demonstrate that automation of the aqua-dag process was possible and then supply four separate proposals with price quotations to robotically automate each of the four manufacturing operations.

I immediately advertised and interviewed a number of machine designers. I temporarily hired a Russian who I sensed had the ability to design equipment. Ev understood the requirements to design a simple machine to simulate a robotic application of aqua-dag by hand cranking the mechanical applicator for coating the neck of a vacuum tube to prove robotic automation was feasible.

I became concerned when Ev stood at his design board for five days without putting one pencil mark on paper. It became obvious his mind and imagination had been working all that time, because when I told him to begin drawing, he drew the machine parts he needed. A machine shop made the parts. Ev assembled the parts and later would demonstrate that automation of the aqua-dag process was achievable.

A morning appointment was scheduled to demonstrate our hand operated aqua-dag machine. We had a twelve-foot circle of Zenith engineers standing around Ev as he proceeded to successfully demonstrate his manually operated machine as it applied the coating to the neck of one of their vacuum tubes. The engineers were satisfied. I then presented our four written proposals with conceptual plan view layout drawings for installing four robotic systems in their plant. Two weeks later I called Zenith and asked about the status of the four proposals that totaled $4.2 million in contracts. I was told I would get at least two of the four robotic contracts.

Great! But nothing happened. I learned that Zenith currently had one hour of labor invested in every TV vacuum tube they made, while the

Koreans were now producing vacuum tubes with 10 minutes of labor per tube. It was obvious Zenith had lost to their Korean competition. I lost hope of ever getting the contracts as promised and had to let both Ev and Mark go. I was unable to secure any more consulting contracts.

U.S. Economic Slump

The U.S. was in a 1980's economic business slump that was affecting many business sectors:

The 1985 oil price slump [1]

Early 1980's recession describes the severe global economic recession [2]

North American video game crash of 1983 [3]

November 21, 1985 Computer slump from overoptimistic forecasting [4]

1985 Semiconductor Slump wasn't over yet [5]

John Deere finds farm equipment slump to be a tough row to hoe [6]

It seemed impossible to keep hoping and trying to get manufacturing consulting contracts during the current bad business climate. My wife was saying, "Donn, there is no money coming in!" In October, 1985, I registered with the Intercristo Christian Placement Network that

---

1 Tulsa World, *tulsaworld.com/business/…slump…./article_bb912cff-9dd*, (accessed August 16, 2015).

2 Wikipedia, *en.wikipedia.org/…/North-American_video_game_crash,*(accessed August 16, 2015).

3 Chicago Tribune, *articles.chicagotribune.com/1985…/business/850320043*, (accessed August 16, 2015).

4 Chicago Tribune. *Articles.chicagotribune.com/…/business/8601120942*, (accessed August 16, 2015).

5 Chicago Tribune. *Articles.chicagotribune.com/1985…/business/850221013*, (accessed August 16, 2015).

6 Chicago Tribune. *Articles.chicagotribune.com/1985…/business/850221013*, (accessed August, 16, 2015).

advertised jobs in nonprofit organizations and listed positions that were open. I quickly approached ten of these organizations and was rejected by all. I concluded maybe my corporate background was not welcome or not going to be a fit with Christian non-profits. Then, in the November issue of Intercristo, one organization listed an Executive Vice President opening. I thought that might be a pretty high reach for me and put the publication aside.

Bible Study & Meditation

My job search was not getting results. I was doing a Bible study meditation one morning late in January, 1986, and will never forget the verses speaking about closed doors that caught my attention. I had experienced many closed doors during the last few months of job searching. Curiously, these verses began by speaking about an open door.

> **"These are the words of him who is holy and true, who holds the key of David. What he opens, no man can shut; and what he shuts, no one can open. I know your deeds. See, I have placed before you an open door that no one can shut. I know you have little strength: yet you have kept my word and have not denied my name."**
>
> **(Revelation 3:7b-8) NIV**

It was obvious I had been unable to open many shut doors. My inner voice asked, "Could it be I ignored an open door that was placed before me? If so, "Thank You, Lord!" Immediately, I recalled the ad for an Executive Vice President. My desk and papers usually are a cluttered mess, so it took me a good while to find the job network publication. It had been almost three months since I had read it, and I was pretty sure the position had been filled by then; but I dialed the phone number anyway.

James who answered the phone was assisting the president for this nonprofit organization. As we talked, he indicated a desire to leave the organization and return to retirement once he helped recruit a qualified person to fill the Executive Vice President position. He said the position was still open and invited me to come the next morning to talk with him and then later to meet with the President. If I was hired, the Board of Directors new organizational design for this non-profit organization would be completed.

,

Part II

STEPPING INTO A NEW CAREER

It was a divine plan that shifted into warp speed to become an experience beyond anything I expected. I joined an organization, made a few staff changes during the first year, then traveled to a number of countries to meet various overseas workers, and worked toward specific mission goals.

> *"No one who puts his hand to the plow*
> *and looks back is fit for the service in*
> *the kingdom of God."*

LUKE 9:62 NIV

Six

FOUR SEQUENTIAL INTERVIEWS

Slavic Gospel Association

I arrived as scheduled at Slavic Gospel Association (SGA); James welcomed me. He explained the executive vice president's responsibilities and catalogued the full range of job qualifications. The job requirements at SGA included managing personnel, budget planning, prioritizing SGA's annual goals within each department, enforcing budget constraints, requiring the use of purchase orders, increasing income, improving coordinated planning of goals and providing leadership to help the president and vice presidents achieve annual goals for the mission.

SGA's president, James said, was an energetic visionary who constantly had new ideas for ways to actualize the organization's effective ministry reach into Russia. Russians had lived under a severe atheistic philosophy of Communism for many years. There was a history of persecution of Russians without any church affiliation and of Christians from both the Russian Orthodox and Protestant churches.

It was surprising to learn that Slavic Gospel Association had never had an executive vice president, but this was not unusual for smaller

31

organizations. Creation of this new position was a Board of Directors decision. James finished interviewing me and made plans for me to meet with the president the next day. Following that interview, the president would schedule a meeting with the organization's seven vice presidents. Then I would be interviewed by the Board of Directors at their next meeting.

Meeting the President

My interview with the president, Peter Deyneka Junior was interesting. He was a tall, slender man with a high level of energy. Evidence of his excitement and enjoyment in this ministry was obvious during our conversation. His father, Peter Senior, had immigrated to the states from Russia in 1914 at age 15. After his departure from his family and homeland, Peter Senior's father, two brothers and two sisters died of starvation under the reigns of Lenin and Stalin.

In Chicago, Peter Senior became associated with several prominent Christian leaders who, over time, led him to Christ and, in 1934, encouraged him to establish a mission to Russia. That mission later became the Slavic Gospel Association. Peter Senior spoke in churches in the U.S., in Communist-occupied European countries and in South America, Australia and Asia. He was known for saying, "much prayer, much power." Peter Junior had succeeded his elderly father and had been the president of the mission for twelve years at the time of my interview. I felt he was a man with whom I could work well.

The Ominous Request

As Peter Junior concluded my interview, he said, "Donn, keep your Ziebell Associates consulting firm alive. There are three of us in our management team who are blacklisted by the Russian KGB. Two vice presidents and I cannot get into Russia because our names are blocked from getting visas." He did not add any more explanation but merely stated it as a fact. He arranged for me to come back in two days to meet with the seven vice presidents.

Meeting the Management Team

The vice presidents consisted of one woman and six men. Their individual oversight of the seven departments included creating Russian Radio Programs, Literature Translation into Russian and Field Ministry, Finance, Russian Information Research, Personnel, Fund Raising, and International Offices. It was their chance to meet me and to learn about my background. They did not have any vote about my being hired. The meeting was congenial, merely a formality affording an opportunity for all of us to meet.

Board of Directors Interview

There were no roadblocks. The Board of Directors planned a meeting at SGA's headquarters the following week. I was invited to attend that meeting for an interview. The Board consisted of sixteen Christian men. Seven of them were involved in other outreach ministries, while the others were business owners or businessmen. A few were retired. Ten of the directors had known Peter Junior for a long time and had served many years on the board. I learned SGA had a 1985 revenue income of $4.3 million and closed the year in the black, but I did not learn any reasons for their establishing the new position of Executive Vice President.

I must have answered all the directors' questions to their satisfaction. At the end of my interview, they asked me to step out of the room. After a few minutes they called me back, informed me of a unanimous vote and said I was hired.

It was explained that I would work under Peter and join him in monthly meetings with the board; and, for some reason yet unknown, I also would answer to the Board of Directors! The Board of Directors meeting adjourned. One board member, a highly respected, nationally prominent gentleman who had served on the board for many years, took me aside and surprised me with advice "I needed to remember." He told me, "Remember, you are now working with Russians. Either they will stand in your way and block progress, or they will move in 100 different directions at once."

On February 6, 1986, I arrived for my first day of work at Slavic Gospel Association.

Seven

My First Few Days with SGA

Peter Junior and I had offices across the hall from one another and shared a secretary. A bit startling was the fact that his office was small, plain and simple, while all other VPs had larger offices. Some had nice furnishings like corporate VPs, i.e., offices with bookcases, pictures on the walls, nice guest chairs and desktops holding different display items. I soon understood that Peter's office mirrored the austerity with which he grew up. As a boy, Peter did not have his own bicycle as did all his friends; they let him ride their bikes.

Peter's character and personality were not focused on the physical world, but on a distant land where people needed to hear the gospel about the God who loves them and values every living soul on earth. Peter's wife, Anita, kept a nice home no different from other people's homes, and she also worked in the mission.

My first priority was meeting individually with the seven vice presidents to get to know him/her and the responsibilities over which they managed.

Finance/Accounting: The woman VP managed this department. Rosemary was a teenager – not a college graduate – when she joined SGA. Peter Deyneka Senior leaned heavily upon her with office duties. He encouraged his employees to gain an education, so Rosemary enrolled in accounting and administration courses at Moody Bible Institute. She impressed me with years of in-house experience and the ability to manage a pretty large task with only three full-time bookkeepers.

Rosemary was glad I arrived, because maintaining financial control within the mission was a constant challenge. This had concerned her. She needed someone above her with a conscientious tenacity to help rein in the spending and instill accountability throughout all mission departments. I recognized her as a very capable person who could help achieve improved financial control of the mission. This was one of the main reasons the position I now held had been created. At the time I am writing this in 2016, I have just attended SGA's retirement party for Rosemary's 50 years of employment – an event now truly rare in today's U.S. workforce.

Russian Radio: Nick was a seasoned SGA missionary, having served many years in Morocco where our Russian radio broadcasts had been created. Several years before my arrival, this function had become a SGA in-house activity. The radio scripts were written in the Russian language, and then voice recorded, edited and supplied to broadcasting stations that transmit the Christian evangelism radio programs beyond the Iron Curtain to the Russian people. Nick's division had a staff of eight people. One was a resident in the Canary Islands, and two others were in Ecuador, South America. Everyone in this department was fluent in the Russian language. Despite the lack of excellent recording studios, they maintained good productivity. A few years after I arrived, we had professionally designed recording studios installed with no 90° room corners, in order to cancel background sound waves, eliminate background noise and provide very high quality recorded radio programs.

Literature Translation/Book Publishing: Roman was educated as a pastor, had excellent Russian language capability, and a great burden for educating Russian believers by teaching inside Russia. He provided educational curriculum for Russian pastors and their leaders to enhance their biblical ministry to their congregations.

Many of the Protestant Church pastors and leaders in Russia had spent time in prison under communism. Many Christians, as well as their children, were politically hindered from receiving good educations. The national school system in the Soviet atheistic culture taught against the belief in God and was very prejudiced against educating children from Christian homes and churches. Roman's mission for this department was focused on translating many Christian books written by over forty-five western authors such as:

C. S. Lewis	C. W. Chesterton	A. W. Tozer
Josh McDowell	Francis Shaffer	J. I. Packer
Don Richardson	Billy Graham	Stephen Gasper

The books were carefully translated into the Russian language, thoroughly proof edited and then printed in large quantities. Once printed, we would find couriers to deliver the books behind the Iron Curtain. The couriers also delivered Russian language Bibles and special Children's Picture Bibles.

Roman's department was made up of five in-house employees and six to eight outside subcontractors with Russian language skills. Roman and his wife, Luba, were a strong team who made trips into Russia. He held small and large teaching conferences for pastors and church leaders, and Luba did the same with pastors' wives and the church women.

Personnel: Jason had one secretary and handled our employee benefits, maintained personnel files and gave a listening ear and counseling to employees as needed. Our small in-house print shop had four workers who published a monthly SGA newsletter. These mailings to SGA supporters kept them abreast of our ministry activities and also served as a public outreach to increase our financial support base. Some of our publications were contracted out to professional printing services. A female supervisor was over the print shop and worked under Jason.

Shortly after my arrival, Jason came to me about the young female who supervised the print shop. She previously was one of our field missionaries. Admittedly, she was very good at her job. She felt she was not properly compensated, which is not an unusual occurrence among employees in nonprofit organizations. Jason and I made a compensation study and found her claim to be true. We gave her a significant increase in salary. Over the following months we identified a few other employees whose salaries needed moderate pay increases. Fixing pay inequities within any organization makes it better managed and more successful.

International Offices: Talking with Andrew was quite a global awakening. SGA had missionary workers in Italy (2), Germany (1), Austria (4), France (1) Ecuador (2), Brazil (1), Paraguay (1), and Argentina (1). Some of them had a spouse or family members with them, as well. Because many Russians migrated to South America after World War II, SGA had created a small Russian Bible Institute in Buenos Aires, Argentina. This school and our activities in Austria, Germany and France were funded within SGA's U.S. budget. Andrew also had a consortium of small international offices or individuals in England, Canada, Australia, France, and New Zealand. These were self-sustaining adjuncts for finding donors to work collectively to minister to the Russian people. All international office leaders attended an international annual conference officiated by Andrew. He alternated sporadic visits to these offices over every two or three years. Andrew's wife, Pauline, also worked full-time as a Russian manuscript proofing editor in the literature department.

Fundraising Development: Bradley managed this department with one secretary and four subordinates. Two employees under Bradley were writers who crafted articles covering SGA's ministry activities, mission achievements, and stories to help both readers and donors stay current with our ministry through our monthly *BreakThrough* newsletter. Our mission's individual projects/program expenditures were covered by our income from tax deductable donations to SGA. Our publications helped people understand SGA's progress in stories told by Russians whose lives had been impacted by our ministry. Information about new ministry opportunities in Russia and appeals to encourage readers to continue their financial support also were included in the publications.

This department also gleaned human interest stories from information from our in-house research department or from stories that leaked out of Russia and came to our attention. I depended upon Bradley for current donor response information and to keep tabs on our on-going income results from fundraising efforts.

Russian Information Research: Orest, our department head, had an earned PhD degree and was fluent in the Russian language. He frequently traveled to Russia to the extent Peter Junior would permit it. Only Orest knew who his contacts were. The risk of his losing access to travel into Russia or causing risks to in-country Russians who trusted their confidentiality with him was extremely important to protect. He worked by himself in intelligence-gathering and was very good at providing regular reports. He regularly had very useful, correct and timely strategic information. We did not ask him to reveal how or from whom it was acquired.

Anita, Peter Junior's wife, was "under Orest" and also worked independently on research. Her interest was more academic in nature. She participated in information-sharing forums and panels about Russia with people from other missions that had ministries inside Russia. She held a very high profile status as an information resource person among the coalition of like-minded missions. She networked closely with the Institute of East West Studies housed in Wheaton College's Billy Graham Library on the Wheaton, Illinois, campus. Our SGA office buildings and the Graham Library shared a common property line that aided her close working relationships.

Both Orest and Anita provided information that played a significant role in the creation of programs and projects for the ministry carried out by SGA inside Russia.

Eight

To gain control of our annual budget it was necessary for Peter and me to meet regularly with all the vice presidents. After talking with Peter, I set the agenda and officiated at each meeting. Everyone was encouraged to participate during our meetings.

According to the Briggs Myer's test, there are sixteen personality types. Our collective management team of nine possessed seven personality types. By expanding to include seven more key subordinates under the VPs resulted with a management team of 16 members possessing ten personality types. Diversity can provide organizational strength when managed well, but conflict can also arise; SGA was not excluded. Visionary driven goal setting frequently requires more financial resources than are available and can produce conflicts.

Budgeting

We reviewed each department's budget plan. Next we reviewed the activities that each VP had within their plan, including expenditures estimated for each of the annual goals. After every department's plan was given a cursory review, it was no great surprise to find that the total of all the plans exceeded our previous year's income by several millions of dollars. Each VP was asked to eliminate the least urgent projects. As the new operating officer, I was aware this request – although expected – would not be received with enthusiasm.

In subsequent meetings, we still had hundreds of thousands of dollars of proposed expenditures we could not fund. It was a painful process, because all of SGA's missionary programs were valued. The vice presidents met together to "horse trade" with one another, striving for a budget that fell within our projected income. Three VPs who had the largest portion of the mission's budget were "men of the cloth." They were pastoral-minded men with great passion for their ministry's activities. I was initially viewed as a businessman who was not yet sympathetic to ministry goals. This was not true; my budgeting experiences had been within three different churches, as well as in several industries.

With everyone working together through numerous meetings, we began to realize our anticipated annual income still could not satisfy everyone's ministry dreams and aspirations. We needed to think more long range. Some projects were deferred to the following year. Others could be started in the current budget year and completed the next year. So a balance between revenue and expenditures was finally hammered out.

Personnel

VP Jason had a passion for helping people and so tended to make over-generous and unrealistic promises to some employees about fringe benefits. I told him this practice had to stop. However, Jason's desire to please employees beyond limits continued. I finally had to terminate him, thus sending a shockwave throughout the mission. This rarely happens in non-profit organizations. Fortunately, Dwight, a mature experienced missionary with solid administrative skills and a gifted personality, had returned from the mission field. He was promoted to VP of Personnel.

Fundraising development

SGA had retained an outside fundraising consultant prior to my arrival. I would ask VP Bradley specific questions about our income performance and other status questions about fund raising activities. He never seemed to have a grasp on anticipated income projections from our fundraising efforts. Everything seemed more dependent on our consultants. We had continued to hover at or slightly above $4 million for the last three years before my hire, without gaining needed income growth. I advised Peter several times over a short time about my observations of Bradley. Soon Peter agreed this was a serious problem, and I terminated Bradley. I did meet with Bradley over lunch a month later to encourage him in his progress of job searching.

I knew of a man who had marketing/sales experience with a heavy equipment manufacturing company and was seeking employment. He was not experienced in nonprofit fundraising, but he impressed me particularly with one of his experiences. He had negotiated the sale of a large earthmoving machine in a third world country. He secured the payment for the sale by accepting 155,000 live goats in exchange for the machine. This was not unusual when selling to the developing world. His firm had a division solely devoted to converting such live stock trades into US dollars by selling the herds. SGA needed dollars - not goats - but Ed demonstrated creative promotional strength.

Ed had an optimistic personality and a good personal work ethic. He was experienced with planning sales forecasts and working toward achieving revenue goals. Surely his background would be a help in increasing SGA's donor revenue. Peter interviewed him and approved my hiring of him. Ed did a fabulous job by increasing SGA's annual income from $4.5

million to $14.5 million over a five-year period. He continued to use our contracted fundraiser to help drive SGA forward by personally directing the fundraising themes for our consultant to use. Ed aggressively added successful targeted fundraising campaigns by promoting the exciting ministry opportunities SGA had in Russia. Additionally, his relationship building and submission of proposals to private foundations that believed in our special projects resulted in receiving millions of dollars of grants from them.

Argentina trip

I traveled to Argentina with VP Andrew to meet with administrators and Board of Directors for the Russian Bible Institute in Buenos Aries. They had been supported by the SGA budget for many years but had failed to initiate adequate fundraising in Argentina. After observing and talking for two days, I had to tell them SGA would begin an annual decrease in their support over the next couple years as they ramped up their own fundraising efforts in the country. They were not very pleased with my visit. Complacency had set in when SGA had undergirded them with financial support for many years. They needed to take the responsibility that is a necessary part of operating a non-profit organization.

Argentina countryside

Achieving control as a team

Everyone at SGA U.S. adapted to an annual cooperative budget planning practice. Establishing the funds required by each department for each of their budget line items became a well-managed standard operating procedure. The use of purchase order requisitions for expenditures on budget line items gave the finance department a "heads up" for payables and ended surprise obligations from unreported verbal contract commitments. Now the excellent departmental monthly financial reports from Rosemary took on a new meaning that helped everyone. Each VP tracked progress within his/her annual planned budget. At the end of my first year, SGA's annual report showed a $40,000 surplus of income over expenditures. Working together, we had become a good management team.

Nine

Germany

Andrew, the VP of International Offices, and I traveled to Germany, where we had a small facility manned by a German citizen who spoke German and Russian. He knew avenues with moderate risk for delivering our printed books and Bibles to destinations inside Russia. It was the first time I met this effective, high energy gentleman who performed a vital role to the success of SGA.

France

I met with the man we supported who operated a small family shop that printed our Children's Picture Bibles in the Russian language. It was said there were some recurring issues with his progress, reliability and financial accountability. A firm but kind stand had to be carefully communicated as to how we would continue to work together.

At another point in my travels, I met an American SGA couple whose focus was on evangelizing Russian immigrants who flowed into Italy in the early1980s. These travelers stayed in Italy for a short time and then traveled on, finally to settle in another European country. The husband reported the number of Russian immigrants arriving in Italy was rapidly declining, because they were using another port of entry into Europe. The couple realized their ministry to the migrating Russians in Italy was ending, and they were planning to retire.

This incident proved the value of visits to distant missionary locations. Situations such as this sometimes occur over an extended time when the home office is uninformed about the status of a missionary stationed abroad who is not under proper oversight or sufficiently accountable to the home office. This happens when some distant missionaries are trusted to live and work independently and do not maintain close contact with mission headquarters. Of course, some fault lies with the person at headquarters who should be in contact with the distant missionary and managing the situation responsibly. This, unfortunately, is not an unusual situation and can occur in any missionary agency. Missionaries who tend to keep their independence and distance are tagged "lone rangers." They need to be committed to regular communication and accountability to headquarters or be terminated.

Austria

Andrew and I split up for different destinations. My next scheduled visit was to our mission office in Vienna, Austria. The woman office manager and another female missionary in this office worked so closely with one another that it was said they were "attached at the hip." Whether this was good or bad was uncertain. Usually, there were one or two male missionaries working out of this office. The office was in touch with an "underground" network of contacts that occasionally provided some helpful information from inside Russia. Their contacts also were part of a network of "shadow" undercover literature couriers.

Before my trip, it was suspected some problem existed in this office. Male personnel did not last long; they would sever their working relationship with our mission. I prearranged to have a meeting with the present office staff of two women and two men. Upon my arrival, I sensed the new executive vice president of SGA was not welcomed by the women!

We sat down around a table in the conference room and began to get acquainted. I wanted to learn about the activities they performed involving Russia. Austria was distanced by several European countries that had common borders with Russia and, therefore, served as a "buffer zone" between Austria and Russia.

About twenty minutes into our meeting, my wooden chair curiously and totally collapsed. I ended up lying on my back on the floor. I did not act upset but instead took the incident in stride. Oddly, this occurrence caused no real excitement or concern to anyone sitting around the table. I could not remember if I had been directed to that chair or it had been the only vacant chair at the time. Another chair was brought to the table, and I again seated myself. The meeting continued a little while longer. The two women did not volunteer much information; the men were rather quiet. Maybe there was nothing important to be shared, which I found very odd for a SGA foreign-based office focused on Russia. As I left that meeting, I felt certain something was wrong, but

I did not know what it might be. I just couldn't identify the problem in such a short time.

When I returned to the U.S., I asked Dwight, the former overseas missionary and now our VP of Personnel, to travel to Austria and spend two or three weeks in the office, just observing. He phoned in and said, "The office is totally dysfunctional." We talked it over and concluded the office should be closed and both women terminated. They were informed we would arrange free individual professional counseling for them stateside to help them with any personal trauma we may have caused by their termination and help them while they sought other employment. The two men were self-supporting missionaries who were secunded to other mission organizations. Thus, we eliminated needless expenditures on the troubled Austrian office.

As promised, both women were kept on the payroll for an extended period. The professional counseling firm spent many months helping them individually. It was discovered the office manager had had a very serious incestuous child abuse history that manifested itself in hatred toward men. That explained why we had experienced the repeated loss of male personnel in the Austrian office.

It hadn't been an easy year, but it was interesting learning more about the extent of SGA's strategic mission network. Then the next year brought something I never anticipated.

Ten

TOURIST TRIP TO MOSCOW AND EASTERN RUSSIA

Constantine and Elizabeth Luschenia were an elderly couple who worked for Slavic Gospel Association. They had emigrated from Russia to the United States many years ago. Now in their 70's, they planned to lead a 1987 tourist trip to Russia. Some friends and supporters of SGA were signing up for the trip.

Peter Junior encouraged me to take advantage of the opportunity for me and my wife, Jean, to go on the trip. He thought it would be a good way for us to learn about the country and culture. It would give me a better understanding of SGA's ministry focus on Russia.

I don't remember how it came about, but we learned that the president of the Baptist Union Church in Moscow had a daughter who was going to be married the next year. Wedding dresses were not readily available or reasonably affordable in the Soviet Union. Jean worked as a consultant in a bridal shop. The shop had an inventory of discontinued or marked down wedding gowns, so Jean selected a wedding gown to take to Russia as a gift for the bride-to-be.

Flying on Lufthansa, we had a short layover in Amsterdam that allowed us to visit the city and view the canals, bridges and old stone buildings along the canals. We saw small boat traffic, as well as occupied houseboats anchored along the sides of the picturesque canals. Flying from Amsterdam, we landed Friday at Moscow's Sheremetyevo International Airport after sunset. The terminal was dimly lit inside, causing the uniformed military guards to appear stern.

Recovery of the luggage was a bit disorganized. We joined other arriving passengers in slow lines until we reached more uniformed men and women who checked our luggage contents, some more thoroughly than others. Constantine told us how he was going to breeze through the luggage check. It became quietly comical to me as the inspectors emptied Constantine's suitcases entirely and made a disarray of the contents. It took him 40 minutes to get through the ordeal, about which he had much to say afterward. We all loaded our luggage onto our tour bus.

Moscow

At 10 p.m., our bus drove us from the airport into Moscow. The overhead lighting on the divided four-lane highway was dimly lit, and hardly a car was on the highway. We were taken to a large hotel on the edge of Red Square. Having experienced the "Cold War" between our countries, our visual impressions of everything were skewed. Women monitors sitting at desks in all the hotel hallways watching people leave or enter their rooms added to our unease. This 24-hour surveillance seemed very curious to us. Jean and I had an eighth-floor room with an excellent view of the Kremlin walls and Red Square. The outside lighting was not bright, but adequate enough to see a few people and an occasional car cross Red Square. The classic, colorful domed St. Basil's Orthodox Church that adorns many photos of Moscow stood in the immediate foreground.

The next day we stood in a long line in Red Square to visit Lenin's tomb. The Russians in line spoke with hushed voices. As we were about to enter the tomb in single file, a military guard instructed us not to speak while inside the tomb. The beauty inside the tomb was impressive. The tops of the walls were decorated with an electrifying pattern of deep maroon polished mineral tile accented with a wide, deep blue azurite stroke like a bolt of horizontal lightning. We walked silently in single file around the glass-encased body of Lenin with his distinctive high bald forehead. He looked like a "wax figure."

On Sunday, our group sat in the balcony of the Moscow Baptist Union Church. We enjoyed the choir. The sermon, as expected, was in Russian. Several hundred parishioners attended the service. The church interior had a modest Protestant design unlike the heavily decorated interiors of the Russian Orthodox Churches.

We toured St. Basil's Orthodox Church and walked through the intricate narrow passages and stairways. The interior design presented an impressive construction of brick work. The exterior ornate design included many multi-colored onion domes.

The Golden Ring

Outside the north Kremlin wall there are stone monuments bearing descriptions about historic leaders and events. Moscow has a 600-mile-long meandering road surrounding it called the Golden Ring. There are sixteen historical towns dating back 1,000 years at varied distances along the route. Each has individualized architectural beauty with buildings constructed out of stones, brick, cement and timber within fortress walls with fortified city gates. The ancient churches and buildings within each Golden Ring town are distinctively different.

Our first Golden Ring bus stop was Vladimir with its historic Golden Gate and Cathedral of the Dormition that dates to 1158. Only the main gate remains from the town's ancient protective walls. Within the cathedral, early princes of Vladimir and Moscow ascended the throne. All the ancient cities provide great opportunities for taking photographs.

Next, we traveled to Suzdal on the Golden Ring. Orest Holovaty pointed through the bus window at a road leading to the east and said, "About 200 miles down that road is a city named Gorky. Russia keeps their political prisoners there. The city is closed to foreigners." Little did I know that Gorky would play a big role in my future!

We were housed in a modern two-story A-frame Intourist hotel with the small Kamenka River flowing behind it. A narrow wooden foot bridge over the river led to a large acreage containing garden plots on the left side of a dirt path. The acreage was quite expansive and extended up to the white walls of the Suzdal Kremlin. To the right of the path were old, well kept, private single-story wood cottages with ornamental cornices typical of old Russian countryside homes. Their exteriors were well-painted with different colors to accent the design of the homes – probably for the visiting tourists. Small gardens, flower beds and a wood fence surrounded each house. The sight of these homes provided a historic rural Russian flavor to our visit. The ancient beauty of everything brought tears of emotion to Jean's and my eyes. A few Russians were working in their vegetable gardens and in the potato field with a view of the Kremlin in the background.

Suzdal was once the religious center of medieval Russia. There the Church of St. Lazarus was built in 1667 by townspeople using funds provided by Grand Princes and tsars. Within their Kremlin walls stood a convent where wives banished by a Prince or tzar lived out their years.

Many churches, a number of typical wood houses and a monastery stood on the grounds. The several museums contained centuries-old artifacts, implements, paintings, furnishings, icons and ancient manuscripts. We saw similar displays when we visited Zagorsk, where the walls of the Trinity Monastery predate 1380. All the towns along the Golden Ring had played their distinct roles in Russia's history. The architecture of the buildings inside each of their Kremlin walls differed from one another in beauty and Russian craftsmanship. My impression was that there were no two churches alike in design among the great number we visited.

Kazakhstan

From Moscow, we flew 2,000 miles east on Aeroflot Airline to Almaty (Alma Ata on some maps), Kazakhstan. The plane's interior was soiled from passenger use. The airline stewardess served us a chicken dinner. None of us could identify what part of a chicken we had. I concluded they threw the de-feathered birds through whirling airplane propellers, which obliterated identification of the cooked chicken portions. The "Archie-Bunker-like" guy in our tour group tried, without success, to get the stewardess to trade his chicken for a waffle. Very little meat could be found on any pieces of chicken our group received.

Disembarking in Almaty, we waited on the airport tarmac by the plane while our luggage was slowly offloaded onto the ground. We were not allowed to take it. We walked to the terminal and then were escorted into an isolated room, thus preventing any contact with local citizens. We waited quite a long while before a bus took us, without our luggage, to the very nice Almaty Hotel. While we waited in the hotel lobby, we noticed that a blonde woman and a dark-haired Asian man lingered in our vicinity. Our luggage did not arrive for two hours!

We could tell that our luggage had been opened and inspected. After we had settled into our rooms, we rode a bus to various war memorials, some with large statues of Lenin, all with well tended flower gardens. All the government buildings displayed the hammer and sickle molded into their concrete facades. The parks were well-groomed. Everywhere we stopped, the blonde woman and Asian man preceded us. It was obvious we were under constant surveillance.

Almaty lies at the foot of the 2000-3000-feet high-snowcapped Zailiski Ala-Tau mountain range. Fresh water from the mountains flows through channels among apple orchards in the city's central park, so every growing tree and plant had lush foliage. In Almaty I saw my first Yurt, a twelve-foot circular, heavy-duty, tent-like hut with the slightly-pointed roof at the center. Outer walls were covered with heavy white canvas with one entry doorway. It is an old dwelling design used in ages past with some still seen on remote landscapes. Late that afternoon, we were to visit a Baptist church. We saw taxicabs, but they ignored us, as we tried to wave them down. It was quite obvious we were being ignored. Then, suddenly, there were no more cabs; it was as though they had disappeared. We saw a man standing by a black car about a half block away obviously watching us. Soon we were able to wave down a few private cars we assumed were made specifically available to us. We split up into several cars and asked to be driven to the church address. One driver indicated he was a physician; but by this time, we had developed a sense that we could not really believe anyone who talked to us. We had a good visit with the church people, who were very surprised by the presence of Americans.

Back at our hotel, Jean and I decided to strike out on our own for an afternoon walking tour of a nearby neighborhood of single-story, old wooden homes that were well maintained but unpainted and weathered. A man stopped us and indicated he wanted to know the time. I showed him my wristwatch; he walked away. Orest explained this Russian practice of asking tourists for the time is designed to make the tourists aware they're being observed.

Our exploration brought us to a large, three-story brick building with many windows and surrounded by a seven-foot-high, wrought iron fence. As we approached, we peered past the open gate and saw nurses. As we continued along the public sidewalk, we saw a person in an open second-story window using a rope to lower a basket down to the ground. A man and woman on the ground placed something into the basket, and it was pulled up and inside the window. To us this seemed to be a clandestine action of some sort. Later Orest told us a family must provide food for hospitalized family members. Hospitals do not have food services for patients.

On our way back to the hotel, we saw people entering a small one-story neighborhood food store, so we entered. About eight customers were waiting for the single clerk working there. There was a sparse quantity of meat behind the slanted class meat counter. Flies were flying around the counter – more than could be counted. On top of the meat counter a 24-count open egg carton tray displayed cracked eggs. Many eggs were missing parts of their shells, thus attracting numbers of flies standing or walking on the exposed egg membranes. We left in utter amazement. We doubted many tourists experienced Russia as we did by venturing back into the neighborhoods.

Kyrgyzstan

The next day our tour group was split into two groups. We flew in two smaller aircraft 350 miles southwest to Frunze, Kyrgyzstan, where we were bused to a small, two-story hotel. An older Asian gentleman with a black armband received us with a hint of hostility. Since the elevator was not working, we carried our luggage to our second-floor rooms. I tripped on one step of the marble staircase. I later discovered that the rise of that step was an inch higher than other steps, most likely a construction error. The windows in our room were wide open without screens. There were no insects at all, since the climate was arid. Oddly, very few people were out on the street and none near our hotel. Possibly an ordinance existed against contact with foreigners.

A small train station on the Russian Railroad stood about 400 feet away from our hotel. I decided to go alone to explore it. As I approached the very plain looking one-story station, I had the odd impression of impersonating Clint Eastwood walking towards a small western frontier train station on a movie set. People inside were waiting quietly for a train. A uniformed military person sat at a small table in the main waiting room, checking people's papers. An armed soldier stood next to him. It was an interesting, yet repressive, sight. It made me recall scenes in the 1965 movie *Dr. Zhivago*.

Our trip leaders had prearranged a visit to a German-Russian Baptist Church. During the Russian Revolution, for national security reasons, many Germans were made to live in the eastern territory of Russia. This was true under Stalin in World War II. A bus driver picked us up, but he would not drive all the way to the church. We had to walk the last several blocks. The choir was in the balcony at one end of the church with a raised pulpit platform at the opposite end of the sanctuary. Our tour organizers, Constantine and Elizabeth, greeted the congregation in Russian. I was called up to the pulpit to extend greetings from the Christians in the United States, with Elizabeth translating my words into Russian. As their choir sang, many in our group, including Jean and I, had tears well up in our eyes; the musical chords sounded so heavenly and moving, despite our inability to understand the words.

Author greeting the congregation   A packed church

When the service ended, the congregation mingled in the church courtyard. Many church members interacted with us. By this time, I had learned that very few people could afford an automobile. Those who did were very challenged to keep them running because of the lack of parts for repairs. I made it known I wanted to meet the man among them who had a car with the most miles. When I was introduced to the older gentleman who owned the car, I presented him with a gift for his car, an expired Illinois license plate in good condition. He treated the gift like gold. Everybody patted him on the back for being recognized as a good automotive mechanic and now with an American license plate.

We broke up in fours and fives to be driven "almost" to our hotel after sunset by a few church people who owned cars. I say "almost," because it was explained to us we would walk the last three blocks in the dark. The drivers did not want to be observed near the hotel with foreigners due to personal concern of being seen in public with Americans. This further proved our hotel was off limits and why there were no people near the hotel. It was to prevent our having contact with the local population. Probably, our trip to the Baptist Church had been officially prearranged by special permission.

The next day we walked to an outdoor marketplace where food and sundry items were for sale. Many large wood fire grills were cooking wonderful smelling shish kabobs of lamb and goat meat but we did not dare to eat any. That evening we carried our luggage to the train station and boarded a night train to travel 2,260 miles "as the crow flies" northwest and past Moscow to St. Petersburg.

Eleven

St. Petersburg, Russia

Traveling west from Kyrgyzstan on a night train does not permit passengers to see any of Russia's landscape. This may be a practice to prohibit tourists and citizens alike from seeing anything, maybe for national security. Russians generally are required to have travel visas to travel out of their areas of residence. I occasionally saw only one or a few lights at great distances away. The train made only a few very quick "whistle stops," usually by a small building and a dimly lit, short wooden train platform where one or two people would board our train.

We arrived in St. Petersburg at daybreak and transferred to a Russian Intourist bus with a young male Intourist guide. The bus took us to a hotel for breakfast. It was an odd breakfast of bread, tea, green peas and hot dogs. Next, we stopped at a Baroque-style Winter Palace on the bank of the Neva River, built in 1754-1762 for the early Tsars. It houses the

Russian State Hermitage Museum. (Search: Hermitage Museum) It was huge and ornate. Sadly, we spent only 90 minutes there and saw a small number of paintings and displays. It is said it would take fifteen years of eight-hour days, spending one minute at every item on display, in order to see everything in the museum.

Next, we visited St. Isaacs Cathedral, which is named after St. Isaac the Confessor, a monk imprisoned in the fourth century by Roman Emperor Valens, but later released. Its construction took place from 1818-1858. Inside, we viewed beautiful pillars covered with the dark blue semi-precious lapis lazuli and others with green malachite mineral. It was visually outstanding. (Search St. Isaac Cathedral) We proceeded to the famous stone Peter and Paul Fortress, built 1706-40 on a small island in the Neva River. The European architecture in St. Petersburg with very huge three-story ornate buildings was evident everywhere along the banks of the Neva River. The buildings created the feeling of walking back many hundreds of years in time to a very sophisticated, stately society.

Interestingly, our young male tour guide showed evidence of being steeped in Communist propaganda. Because Russian citizens have difficulty acquiring private telephones, he indicated we Americans did not have access to private telephones, either. He said the U.S. had an incomplete distribution of available health care for our citizens, but the Russians were more fortunate to have socialized medicine. The guide was an annoyance to my wife. One man in our group played the role of an annoying Archie Bunker-type of guy. He gave the tour guide a conversational fit. But the tour guide would not believe anything we told him about the United States, thinking it to be US propaganda.

We visited some spectacular Russian historical landmark buildings, but the most unbelievable one was the Summer Palace of Peter the Great (See views via internet), completed in 1723. The massive size, with its interior design, gilded room moldings, extensive parquet floors in huge ballrooms and dining halls, is breathtaking. Equally massive is the outdoor landscape: an enormous back portico and wide staircases with cascading water flowing down into extensive reflecting ponds, all displaying numerous gilded statues, along with soaring water fountains adjacent to walkways through flower gardens with a well-planned assembly of trees. It is an impressive, romantic-like experience that one leaves reluctantly.

Estonia

A chartered bus took us into Tallinn, Estonia, a Baltic nation. Tallinn is the capital city on the Gulf of Finland shoreline. There we had an informative female Estonian tour guide. The country was still under Russian domination, as evidenced by their flag's Hammer & Sickle, but they were in the process of becoming independent again. However, the suppression by the Russians was still evident. We visited an Estonian Baptist Church. In Slavic Gospel Mission headquarters before this trip I was given an American's name to be passed along to an assistant of the senior pastor, which I did. While the senior pastor did not meet us when visiting his church, we were given an invitation with directions to come to his house; we were cautioned, "Come after dark and please practice silence while walking to my address."

We had a gracious visit with the pastor and family. He explained how communist rule had oppressed and threatened him and his congregation. But that was soon to come to an end since regime change was beginning to happen in the Baltic nations. We gave the pastor some Christian books Slavic Gospel Association had published for pastors in Russia and occupied nations.

In Tallinn, our guide took us to the large sports arena, of which the citizens were proud, then onto a log cabin out in some remote woods. It was a historical site similar to the log cabin sites scattered around our states, representing the bare essentials of the frontier lifestyle that existed with the western expansion of the US.

Latvia

Latvia, also a Baltic nation, was the next country we visited. It also had been under communist control. We arrived at a tall hotel in Riga, the capital city located on the Gulf of Riga, and waited for our rooms to become available. When given permission to proceed to our assigned rooms, we learned that the elevator was broken; so we lugged our luggage up many flights of stairs. On an outdoor walking excursion to a nearby park area, we observed a man standing at a bus stop wearing a four-foot diameter circle made with wire. It held many rolls of toilet paper spindled on the wire and hung around his neck and shoulder like a bandolier. He had made a sizable purchase, because toilet paper was not regularly available.

That evening we went into a large, tall Nordic-like church with high ceilings and wood arches. It was a Protestant church that housed the third-largest pipe organ in the world. When it became known we were Americans, we became a small spectacle to the people around us who had come for the organ concert. The music lasted well over an hour before we returned to our hotel.

We returned to Moscow in preparation to leave the country on Lufthansa Airline. We had time to go to a park-side plaza overlooking the University of Moscow. Sidewalk vendors were there to haggle over prices of items they were selling to tourists. I purchased a Russian Red Army belt and buckle. But, unfortunately, Russian military luggage inspectors at the airport confiscated it during my baggage check prior to departure. I had the strong feeling I had been observed making the purchase at the plaza and that airport baggage inspectors most likely had been tipped off that I had a Red Army belt. They did, however, miss the Russian Navy belt and buckle I had purchased earlier during our trip.

Back home in the United States and returning to work, I wrote a trip report about my observations and experiences in Russia and submitted it to my boss, SGA's President, Peter Deyneka Junior. My daily work with the mission kept me busy, and the weeks seemed to fly by.

Meanwhile, as always, Peter's mind was constantly formulating ideas about our mission activities inside Russia. Unknown to me, he had given much thought to one of his ideas. The challenge for a special life-changing project would soon be presented to me to determine if it could be achieved.

Twelve

Peter and I regularly met together to discuss mission activities. One day he changed the subject. "Donn, as you know I am blacklisted by the KGB, as are Andrew and Nick. We are not allowed to enter Russia. I asked you to keep Ziebell Associates registered as an Illinois business. I would like you to design a business seminar program under your company's name and prepare a proposal that can be submitted to Russian authorities. They may approve it, thus allowing you to enter Russia and open another door for our ministry."

What an interesting challenge! My position in SGA would not allow me to be the only person leading the seminars. Additionally, I needed a diverse team of people experienced in a variety of business disciplines with business topics that each man would be qualified to teach if he was attracted to this opportunity. There was an immediate response of interest by those to whom I presented this opportunity. As a result, the proposal contained the following seminar topics:

Seminar Leader's specialization	**Seminar topic**
Metallurgical Engineer	The Four Factors of Production
Electrical Engineer	Electronic Controls for Automated Manufacturing
Business Administration	Sales/Marketing Products & Capital Goods
Manufacturing Management	Survey of Important Manufacturing Issues
Mechanical Engineer	Material Handling of Raw Materials
Quality Control	Science of Plastics in Manufacturing
Packaging Consultant	Packaging Products for Consumers & Manufacturers
Business Administration	Manufacturing Organizations & Systems
Business/Finance	Computer Modeling–Export & Import
Market Research	Market Research for Improving Business Results

The seminar would be held in the mornings, break for lunch, and then regroup for a manufacturing plant tour. It was hoped we could identify at least one plant production process that possibly needed improvement. Then the following morning it could be discussed in the class before the presentation of the scheduled seminar topic.

Orest, VP of Research, had a fair number of contacts in Russia to help him select individuals with whom seminar opportunities may exist. The business seminar proposal was completed on July 19, 1989, and Orest took three copies into Russia. He gave the proposal to three Russians thought to be aggressive enough to pursue the idea. One man was Dr. Vladimir Kalmykov, Professor of English at the Dobrolyubov Institute of Foreign Languages. Unknown to me was that I would be in Moscow the fall of 1989 attending the Moscow International Book Fair to help man our SGA display booth for which SGA had received official approval.

Thirteen

THE 1989 MOSCOW BOOK FAIR

Moscow began sponsoring International Book Fairs in 1977. Some of the fairs had special focuses such as fiction, nonfiction, children's literature and masters' classics, as well as other genre. I was unaware of the plan but was surprised when I learned SGA was assigned floor space in Moscow's 1989 International Book Fair. Despite being the Executive VP for two and a half years, there remained a tendency for Russian-speaking staff to work "close to their vest" on like events until they decided I needed to know their plans. I refused to let it bother me, and I smiled inwardly, remembering that, when I was hired, one Director took me aside and clued me in to how Russians can act sometimes.

Truthfully, there was one day when all the events in SGA were troubling enough to cause me to question myself. "Am I correct that this is the job God really meant for me to have?" I remember how I found confirmation that it was. I listed all the actions and interview steps, each with a 50/50 chance, that had to be a "Yes" in order to be hired. The mathematical compounded probability was. 0.004. This very small number meant the likelihood I would get the job was zero. I then knew with certainty God specifically placed me in my position. Never again did I doubt it.

Peter Junior said I would join him, Roman, Andrew, Eugene and Orest at the book fair. I was surprised Peter and Andrew were permitted entry into Russia for the book fair.

While in Moscow, I had the opportunity to ride on the subway system. It is the most impressive and beautiful system I have ever seen (versus Chicago, London and Tokyo). Each Moscow subway terminal has a different architectural design using tile, marble, pillars and outstanding statuary and very long rising escalators. It was very clean. Anyone would enjoy a self-guided architectural tour through their subway terminals; or even by viewing them on the internet. They're unbelievable!

The Fair

The exhibits were designed with a barrier along the aisle in front of each booth with an entry gate that could be controlled to limit the number of fair attendees inside a booth at any one time. This allowed us to "keep tabs" on our Christian literature and Bible displays. While I did not speak Russian, those in our team fluent in Russian engaged people in faith-focused conversations. The challenge was to discover a person's sincere spiritual interest versus those just looking for anything that was free. A sincere person would leave with one or two free books that would best complement his or her interests.

Orest gave me advance notice; "Donn, one day during the Book Fair, a certain gentleman's smiling face looking at you will appear in the crowd standing outside of our booth. He is a professor and will make contact with you. He will be the sponsor of your proposed seminar program and probably want to speak with you outside so your conversation won't be overheard. This was the first I learned that I would meet anyone inside Russia who was acquainted with my proposal.

Surprised by walking around

Because I did not speak Russian I wasn't much use in SGA's booth. I spent some time walking around and looking at other booths and making general observations. I came upon one very long single-file line of Russians and began walking toward the head of the line to see what held their interest.

Soon I came upon something I would not have expected. The line went right past an American booth tended by the famous American atheist Madelyn Murray O'Hair, who, along with her son, had come to promote atheism to the Russians. The Russians were already very much indoctrinated in the philosophy that there is no God. Interestingly, none of the Russians would engage her in conversation. They were not interested in anything she had to offer and ignored her. I took several pictures of her in her booth. One photograph captured her putting her hand up towards me as a signal to stop taking her picture. I was able to capture a good picture of her later.

I continued to follow the line to see what handout the Russians were patiently waiting to receive. Turning the corner, I found they were more interested in getting a free pencil than anything Madelyn Murray O'Hair had to offer. Now years later, while writing this book, I came across a similar report written by Tim Cavanaugh for "The Corner" section in the National Review published on February 28, 2016: ". . . the high profile of evangelical Christianity in the Ronald Reagan era demonstrated even to O' Hair that she was on the losing side of history. The final insult came in 1989, when the Moscow Book Fair crowd ignored her atheistic literature while grabbing 10,000 free New Testaments."

The Professor

One afternoon the smiling face of a gentleman appeared in the crowd. His eyes, steadily focused on me, signaled he was the man Orest mentioned. I judged him to be in his 40's. He was Dr. Vladimir Kalmykov, a professor who was teaching in a foreign language institute in the city of Gorky. He spoke English very well.

We ate a meal together in a restaurant on the exhibition grounds, and then he suggested we go outside for a walk to get better acquainted. We exchanged gifts, a Russian art book from him and a solar calculator and a U.S. news magazine from me. Afterwards, in the fashion typical of living in a former police state, he wanted to go to a location farther away from the American pavilion and other people to discuss the seminar proposal. The weather was chilly outside. We walked away from everyone until we were sure we could not be heard. This made me feel like an undercover secret agent.

Response to the Proposal

He was very well acquainted with my seminar proposal. In fact, I was quite surprised when he requested changes to the list of topics in my proposal:

Delete	Add
Material Handling	Contract Writing
Electronic Automation	Business Law
Packaging	Taxation
	Import/Export Agreements

He said someone in the KGB in Gorky wanted to change some seminar topics, which seemed odd. But I learned much later that some education authorities, most likely in Moscow's Ministry of Education, were the ones trying to exert their wishes to "gain personal self-satisfaction." It was my guess he had to report the outcome of his negotiation for changes to the seminar topics.

Although Vladimir suggested good topics, I explained I had no idea where I would find seminar leaders who were experienced practitioners in the suggested areas of interest. I explained that my seminar leaders were all full-time employees who worked out the ability to come to Russia using their own vacation time and were unable to take unpaid leave from their jobs to lead the seminars. He understood and seemed satisfied that, at least, he had attempted to change some of the topics. The seminar proposal had already moved through state and local Communist Party channels, including the KGB. That Gorky was closed to foreigners was a well-known fact. Vladimir said one more approval still was needed from the Ministry of Higher Education in Moscow.

I brought up the fact that seminar leaders would also use a Bible verse that related to their topic and that I wanted to offer each seminar attendee a Bible as a gift. They could leave their copy at the Language Institute for the students, if they so desired. He said he would send a communication to me granting permission to bring the "text books" into Russia. A few biblical examples of what the seminar leaders had planned were:

Four Factors of Production Contained in a Parable: Matthew 21:33-34
Accurate Scales and Weights and Measures: Proverbs 11: 1 & 16:11
God Quality-Control-Tested His Creation of the World: Genesis 1:4, 10, 12, 18 etc.
A person Given Opportunity and Resources is Accountable: Luke 12: 42, 48
Business Law as Found in the Book of Proverbs

Vladimir and I spent a several hours together and enjoyed one another's company. He believed the program would be accepted as proposed. I assumed from the approval process that the seminar program would take place in Moscow, since that is where we had met. In March, 1990, I received a FAX from him that approval was secured and that a visa invitation would follow.

Part III

ENTERING GORKY THE EXILE CITY

*"Travel within the Soviet Union was
restricted even for Russians. They needed
internal visas to travel outside their places
of residence. As for foreigners, it was rare
that we could get such permission, . . ."*

A REPORTER'S LIFE
WALTER CRONKITE

Fourteen

Moscow to Gorky by Land

Mikhail Gorbachev served as General Secretary of the Communist Party in the Soviet Union from 1985 until 1991. He served as the country's head of state from 1988 until USSR's dissolution of states in 1991. Gorbachev's policies of *glasnost* ("openness") and *perestroika* ("restructuring") and his reorientation of Soviet strategic aims contributed to the end of the Cold War. He removed the constitutional role of the Communist Party for governing the union of states, which inadvertently led to their dissolution in the Soviet Union.

During what was a major reorganization of Russia by Gorbachev there was a freeing spirit for change within the nation and people at large. My proposal for providing business seminars by U.S. businessmen was submitted at an opportune time. I did not realize the timing was so perfect in Russia's history. Quite probably, had it not been for Gorbachev's time in Russia's history, my seminar proposal would never have been considered.

Official Invitation

Ziebell Associates' seminar proposal had been in the hands of Russian decision-makers for nine months. I received a written approval by TELEFAX in the Russian language on June 27, 1990.

The Translation:

We are happy to invite you to the city of Gorky, USSR, from 24 May through 4 June, 1990, in order to conduct, under the auspices of GSP I FL*, seminars for the management staff of enterprises dealing with production management and external economic activity.

Your stay in the USSR (salary, room and board, travel within the USSR, etc.) Will be fully covered by the funds of the cooperative "Polyglott" ** at GSP I FL.

To obtain a visa please apply to the nearest Consular Department of the Soviet Embassy in the USA.

Signed by Dean G. P. Ryabov and stamped with an official seal

*Gorky State Pedagogical Institute of Foreign Languages
**The organization Dr. Kalmykov created to sponsor the seminars

Official Visa Confusion

I was amazed that Gorky, an exile city for Russia's political prisoners and closed to foreigners, was the city where the seminars would be held. But I had to delay the start date to early August. No doubt that USSR's Washington, D.C., Embassy was conflicted by changes happening in Moscow's bureaucracy. Things seemed to have turned upside down for them concerning Gorky. This city historically had been closed and off limits to foreigners for many years, and now they received my request for a visa to Gorky. Really? It never had happened before.

Russia's Embassy in Washington D.C. would issue a visa to me for Moscow, but not for Gorky. This obstacle made me calmly excited and intrigued about what I and my other seminar leaders might experience in Gorky, if and when we arrived there. On top of this, I had also requested Dr. Kalmykov to allow me to travel the 250 miles from Moscow east to Gorky by land and not by plane or train.

Still, my nerves were tested as I received my visa to Moscow only fifty minutes before checking in at Chicago O'Hare's International Airport check-in counter. Associate George Laybourne received his visa two hours before check-in. The other associates received visas between one and several days before departure. It was a case of learning about the Soviet operating procedure while still in the U.S.

Bureaucracy Tested

With only a Moscow visa, I landed at Moscow's Sheremetyevo International Airport and was met by Dr. Vladimir Kalmykov, and Michael Dashkov and Victor Fitov, both of whom who would be my two principle translators, and their Asian van driver. Their first task was to acquire the official visa in Moscow to allow me to enter Gorky after we traveled by road to get there. This became a quiet comedy for me to witness. After four hours of visiting many "official" offices my hosts could not acquire any visa to Gorky.

Moscow's elite "cast" system became apparent to them. My companions concluded the Muscovites were treating them like poor cousins from the countryside outside of Moscow's city limits. It was late afternoon, and, now defeated, they forgot about the land visa and decided they could get the visa issued right in Gorky where they personally knew the authorities. This meant we would take the chance we would not get stopped on our journey by road. Fortunately, I tend to like risk and suspense and now, more so, in Russia.

Blind-man's Bluff

After failure with Moscow's bureaucrats, the evening was upon us; it was now dark. The plan was to take me to an elderly widow's high rise apartment on the outskirts of Moscow. The woman had agreed to house an American in a spare room for one night. In the dark with a minimum of street lighting, my companions tried to find the apartment building. We drove around, around and around without finding the address. The men finally explained their dilemma: the Russian's Cold War homeland defense method was to screw up any enemy invasion attempt by scrambling the apartment and house numbers out of numerical sequence to confuse occupying foreign military. But now we were like the enemy, unable to find the woman's apartment. It took two hours of continual searching.

Finally, upon arrival, the woman silently waved me in and directed me to a clean room and closed the door. I went to bed and tried to sleep – "tried" because her apartment windows were wide open, and the mosquitoes were as bad as the Japanese air attack on Pearl Harbor! In the morning, I thanked the woman with one of the few Russian words I knew and gave her a Christian book, *Tongue in Check* by Joseph M. Stowell, in Russian.

No Room in the Inn

The next night in the ancient city of Vladimir, the hotel clerk would not rent a room to me because I did not have a ground visa permitting me to be in their city. She also said I looked much too young for the birth date listed in my passport! Kalmykov knew a former student in the city who arranged for his father-in-law to welcome me to stay in his apartment. The man was an emotionless, retired English-speaking Red Army Officer who, of course, had never had an American in his home. It proved to provide for a very interesting discussion about faith in God and Jesus Christ.

My host's son, Anton, immediately got permission to stay one day behind his class of Red Army inductees because of "an American staying with them that night." I autographed a New Testament for Anton. It later was reported to be of great interest to his fellow inductees. I left several Christian books in Russian for the former Red Army Officer, who also was reported to be enjoying them.

Road Trip Eastward

I cannot remember when, if or where we ate as we drove across the vast countryside. I was enthralled as we traveled along a "grade C-minus highway" through small, distantly-spaced rural villages with single-story "*Fiddler-on-the-Roof* "-like wood homes. Dodging holes and bumps was a constant norm. What was striking was that my four companions treated me as an American Christian who should have all the answers to their uninterrupted flow of sincere questions. It was like an evangelist's perfect dream to be a witness about one's faith in Jesus Christ. I never expected this to occur so suddenly inside Russia. Plus I would be with three of these men for three weeks. What an opportunity!

Knock, Knock!

"If you are a stranger traveling anywhere in our country you can stop and knock on any door, and you will be shown a welcomed hospitality," said Dr. Kalmykov." Do you want to do that?" I said, "yes." Pulling up to a house among houses on both sides of the village roadway, he knocked on a door." We have an American with us; may we come in?" Well, from their response, I felt welcomed like a terrestrial visitor. "They want to know if you would like a cup of tea?" I said that would be nice.

Russian couple with American visitor

When I saw the huge hospitality cup of tea, I immediately realized my bladder already felt full. But I drank it slowly, as I gave them several different copies of prominent western-authored Christian books translated into Russian. They were quite delighted with the books. I assumed they could read, because Russia is supposed to have a population with one of the higher literacy rates in the world. I used their preoccupation with the books to get directions to their indoor "outhouse" on the back wall of their enclosed back porch.

After a 45-minute visit, we departed and vanished eastward down the highway toward the horizon. The Christian books were left with a very surprised family. The only proof they had to show their neighbors that an American had visited their home would be the books that could be shared with them.

The Name Changed

My second day in Russia traveling overland by car the remainder of the 250 miles was a great experience. Interestingly, just two days before, I had left Chicago O'Hare Airport with the intended ultimate destination to be Gorky, Russia. But that is "not exactly" where I arrived. So how on earth did I find myself in a city named Nizhny Novgorod instead?

I discovered that, during my journey from the U.S. to Gorky, the city's name was changed back to the ancient name Nizhny Novgorod. Gorky was named after their writer Maxim Gorky (1868 – 1936), an author nominated five times for the Nobel Prize in Literature. He was also a Socialist opposed to the Tsarist regime and for a time closely associated with Vladimir Lenin. The reinstated ancient name Nizhny Novgorod literally means "*Newtown the Lower,*" since it was located downstream from Yaroslavl, northeast of Moscow, on the Volga River. I enjoyed the road trip, but all the Ziebell Associates who would follow me to present seminars months later would travel from Moscow to Nizhny Novgorod by night train.

Fifteen

First Impressions in Nizhny Novgorod

The city is ancient (1221 AD), historic and militarily strategically located on a high embankment above where the Oka River flows into the Volga River. The Volga begins in Yaroslavl, 150 miles northeast of Moscow, becoming a large waterway that allows boat travel and trade for 2,193 miles through the heart of Russia to the Caspian Sea. I was given a big room with a high ceiling in the old Russia (Ru-see-ah) Hotel for my stay in the city. It stood close to the Kremlin at the same high elevation. My windows provided a great view of the Volga River with its active river traffic at a distance below.

It was mid August 1990 when I arrived. All grammar school girls celebrated the first day of school by wearing large, wide ribbon bows on top of their heads. The Russia hotel was a five-minute walk to the city's walled Kremlin. Housed within its walls were the administrative office buildings for the entire Nizhny Novgorod region. Frequently, I entered the gate in the Kremlin wall facing the city to tour the grounds and look at the buildings and a monument. Inside the gate and immediately along one wall, there was an outdoor display of Soviet WW II armament.

Hotel room mornings

Dr. Kalmykov acquired my city visa permit without any problem. At his request, he and my two translators, Michael Dashkov and Victor Fitov, arrived at my hotel room after breakfast to listen and learn more about the Protestant Christian Faith. I had given each of them a Russian language Bible. My first surprise came after I drew a horizontal line on paper and then added a "B.C." at the left and an "A.D." at the right end of the line. I placed a cross at the center of the line to represent the place on the timeline when Jesus Christ was crucified. I told them the Old Testament was written during the time to the left of the cross and the New Testament to the right of the cross. That made an unusual impression upon them; they had not seen a representation like that before. So, every morning of the that first week, we spent an hour covering passages they read in their Bibles; they had many questions.

On our second morning, professor Kalmykov told me his 16-year-old daughter Anna, would not read and that he and his wife, Galya, would do her homework. I gave him a copy of an Illustrated Children's Bible as a gift for Anna. The next morning, he arrived in my hotel room and said that a miracle had happened. Anna started reading the picture Bible and continued to read it until 3 a.m. He was so surprised and pleased he could not stop talking about how he and his wife were so amazed by her response.

Chilled to the Bone

The August weather was already quite chilly. I was cold, because I did not have warm clothing. The next day Michael brought one of his father's sweaters for me to wear for the duration of my stay. But I still got chilled to the bone. I decided that evening to run a hot bath in my hotel bathroom to warm my bones. With great anticipation, I started filling the cold tub, only to discover that I did not have any water that was more than slightly lukewarm. I continued to be very aware that my bones felt cold, but I could not let that stop me.

Sightseeing in Gorky

My three companions were occupied with their daytime duties during the week. This gave me time to walk around portions of this old city that had been named Gorky until one week ago. While part of Gorky was down at the Oka and Volga River level, the older city and Kremlin were on high ground elevated hundreds of feet above the rivers for better defense in ancient times. In less than ten minutes I could walk from the hotel, past the Kremlin to enter the city. It is reported that within the city there are over six hundred historical architectural and cultural monuments. Between my hotel and the Kremlin, I would walk past a statute of a famous aviator standing on the hill near the highest tower in the Kremlin wall and overlooking the Volga River

The downtown area was accessible with a short walk, and one could get around easily by walking. None of the city buildings were over three stories. A bus system allowed people to travel from the outlying residential areas. Taxis were available but had to be scheduled by phone. After Dr. Kalmykov called for a cab, one would arrive, hopefully, within a half hour or less or never show up at all. In some places, there were nice lawns in parks with black iron fences, all which were well maintained. Occasionally there would be a person with an old-world style straw broom sweeping a street. Under communism, that person was given equal respect for his/her assigned task in society. Typical of Europe, beautiful fresh cut flower arrangements were on display for sale along the sidewalks. Vases of flowers graced many homes I had the privilege to visit. I happened upon the statue of the Russian author Maxim Gorky standing facing a breeze with a shoulder cape slightly caught by the air.

Time with Victor

Victor was the only Russian I met who owned an automobile. The car was kept in a rented garage a mile from his apartment. One day, he wanted to show me a store that sold consumer goods. Inside the store were large buckets, plastic flowers, pruning knives and other items not needed. He said, "Look around; there is nothing here that we really need. What we need are soap and other common daily products that can be used." He took me to a meat market where people stood in line. He went to the head of the line and purchased a pre-ordered Czar fish for us to have for dinner at his apartment. Victor was an instructor of navigation for the Inland Waterways Institute. His actions at the meat market signaled to me that he was of a certain social status that afforded some priority over that of the general Russian population. Communism never made everyone in society equal as Socialism claims to do.

The lack of adequate consumer goods was common. Frequently, a man or a woman was seen on a city sidewalk with used plumbing parts, faucets or locks by their feet. Patiently, they waited for a buyer who needed the exact item on display. Victor took me to his small, three-bedroom apartment that was on the second floor of one of the common, all-concrete, 10-story apartment buildings. He lived with his wife, two teenage daughters and his elderly mother and father. They treated me as one of the family. My relationship with this family became very close. Still, I can admit that a Czar fish, although considered a delicacy in Russia, is extremely full of bones and quite greasy.

Things Quickly Learned

One thing I learned very fast – whether in a hotel bathroom, a private bathroom or in any business, school or apartment – was used toilet paper is not flushed down the toilet. Rather, it is deposited in a container provided next to the toilet. Apparently, their waste treatment system could not handle paper refuse.

Outside of the apartment buildings, large above ground steam pipes wrapped in insulation traveled from the central heating plants and into the apartment buildings. No apartment has its own heating system, but rather taps into the central heat supply piped into the building.

These tall apartment buildings contained no elevators. Two flights of stairs separated each floor in the buildings. An 18-inch diameter steel pipe in the stairwell extended from the top floor down to the ground level. Opening a door on the pipe at each floor allowed garbage to be deposited. It fell straight to the bottom, where it accumulated for disposal. Unfortunately, this convenience provided a bit of an odor in the entire ten-story stairwell.

A Cab Ride

One afternoon Dr. Kalmykov ordered a cab to go across the Oka River to a trade show. I was the first American the cab driver had seen. His response was to refuse payment for our ride. Because he was speeding, a policeman stopped him. Our driver's excuse was that he had an American in his cab. The policeman stuck his head into the cab. I said, "How are you doing?" He snapped his head back out of the cab and told the driver to proceed. The Russians with me all laughed at the policeman's reaction.

I felt very safe walking around in Gorky. Common to all Europe, there would occasionally be Gypsies with children in tow pestering pedestrians by begging for money. I was surprised by Victor's wife, Luda, telling about trusting a Gypsy to hold one of her five ruble notes while the Gypsy told her fortune. Surprisingly, during the encounter, the five-ruble note disappeared and she could not get it back. Upon arguing with the Gypsy, Luda was told that if she didn't let her alone, the woman would make her rings disappear also. This scared Luda, and she returned home very mad. Luda was a smart woman and I was surprised that she had been tricked by the Gypsy.

Cultural Exposures

A language translator I met said that, as a young man, he had served for a few years as some type of Russian advisor in an African country. He claimed he had become familiar with the Bible during that time. However, it did not seem evident to me that he had read it. He surprised me by asking whether it was okay for a Christian to have another woman involved in his life in addition to his wife. I told him "absolutely not." He was not very favorable to my answer.

My translator, Michael Dashkov, had been a member of the Communist Youth Organization and was reported to be an excellent gymnast in his former days. That gave credence to my hosts' assurance they could acquire my Gorky visa through their connection with authorities in Gorky.

The Russian Orthodox Churches were quite prevalent with beautiful, ornate architecture inside and out. Usually I only saw older people inside the churches. Many of the women would have small children with them. I saw an occasional elderly man, but I never observed any worshippers who were in their teens, 20's or 30's and no middle age men.

One man invited me to his apartment. We were alone, so he took out a tiny altar and something that looked like a prayer book from a hiding place. His secrecy reminded me of the fear of persecution of any Christian believer discovered in the atheistic Communist regime. It was even more of a fear if one held a position of status in a government state-run industry, agency or organization. My host said he worshipped all alone and prayed often. He was conveying that he was a devout Christian believer within the Russian Orthodox Church.

Sixteen

BUSINESS SEMINAR DAY ONE

During my first week in Nizhny Novgorod my host Dr. Kalmykov took me to the Dobrolyubov Foreign Language Institute and introduced me to the Dean. We looked at the classroom where we would be conducting the seminar during my second week in Nizhny Novgorod.

I wondered why the Ziebell Associates' Business Seminar proposal had been accepted. My host's explanation was brief: "things are changing." Much later, I learned that President Gorbachev was shaking things up in Russia. The Nizhny Novgorod State University published the following: "Today it is the 'test site' for democratic reform and free market initiatives. If transition to a peaceful, democratic future is to occur in Russia, Nizhny Novgorod will be the pacesetter. You are a first-hand witness to a unique historical phenomenon, a society moving from totalitarianism to democracy with all its ups and downs, joys and sorrows." [1]

This published notice was unknown to me and my associates. It is not known if it was published before, during or after we held our seminars.

---

1 "Welcome to Nizhny Novgorod," Nizhny Novgorod State University. http://www.unn. runnet.ru/nn/. Date unknown, (accessed. May 17, 2016).

But the experiences we had surely indicated we were the first Americans to enter this "test site" planned to achieve societal change toward a free market democracy. Now, in 2016, when I am writing this, I view that exciting announcement as having have been a little over-optimistic, considering how things in Russia have transpired since 1990.

Seminar Start-up

The seminar week would be busier than I had imagined. Gorky, now renamed Nizhny Novgorod, is listed as Russia's third, fourth and fifth largest city. I concluded "fifth largest" may be correct. It was closed to foreigners from 1959 to 1991. Yet, interestingly, the seminar program approval allowed me to enter the city in August of 1990.

Monday morning, Dr. Kalmykov accompanied me to the language Institute. On our way there, he said he expected some KGB personnel would be among the attendees. That did not surprise or bother me. A crowd of 60 or more, mostly men and only a few women, filled the lecture room. They all appeared to range from their late 50's to possibly their late 70's. My plan for each day was to have a morning seminar session and then have the group visit a manufacturing plant in the afternoon.

Two weeks before leaving the States, I had faxed a simple easel design to Dr. Kalmykov for holding a visual flipchart teaching aid. I was assured it was ready the day before the seminar. Now a 30" x 30" square board without legs was delivered, along with a hammer and two nails. Suppressing shock, I dragged a table in front of the podium, stood the board on it, and used my briefcase to hold the bottom of the board to keep it from sliding on the table as it leaned against the podium. After driving the two nails partially into the board, I hung the flipchart on the nails. I felt I efficiently handled this surprise. Could this be my introduction to how preparations are handled in Russia? On second thought, maybe the Russians just wanted to see how an American would respond to an unexpected challenge while they watched!

Dissimilar Career Paths

After I was introduced, it seemed best to start by describing my career path that had included working for six different corporations in very different manufacturing industries. As I reached the point of talking about my fourth career step, a low buzz began, with some in the class exchanging comments among themselves. I stopped and asked my translator what was being said. "They say you are a butterfly!" At that moment, the comment didn't clarify anything for me, so I continued. But much later I learned their early perception of me was that I was unstable and, therefore, hopped around from job to job. To Americans, this was a common way of broadening our career experience, which would be valuable to each subsequent employer and would increase our value for marketing ourselves for changing jobs.

However, my career changes were completely contrary to the Russian experience. Men and women in Russia spent their whole lives working for just one employer, resulting in making them familiar with only one industry. They did not have job mobility. So, "being a butterfly" in their view, was not a positive. It was a bad way to start the first seminar. Nevertheless, it was "water over the dam." They would learn that employment changes would be true of most of the following seminar leaders and a rather common pattern of employment in the United States.

Classroom Interaction

Despite being a butterfly, I continued by focusing on an overview of the seminar programs that would be presented in the following months. Then I got into my topics of value added manufacturing, the four factors of production, and alternate approaches to solving manufacturing plant problems. I also covered manufacturing issues including people's changing values, authority, implementation of technological change and cost measurement.

As I was presenting these topics I tried to start a dialogue with the audience; but it did not work. Their culture was like many other world cultures: the student remains silent and learns from the speaker. But by the end of the first morning, I had begun to get a little bit of audience response and participation, which improved by the end of the week. By achieving this, I made it a classroom norm that my associates would be able to enjoy from their seminar dialogue with the attendees.

Lunch Recess and Surprise

We broke for lunch. Everyone went his own way with the plan to reconvene afterward and travel to a manufacturing plant. The intention was that together we would be able to observe something in the plant that might be improved and, thereby, enable a discussion and exchange of ideas. I was disappointed when only nine individuals showed up for the first plant tour at a shoe manufacturing plant. This response is best explained by the fact that people worked in one industry their whole life, so they had no curiosity, interest or motivation to learn anything about another industry that would have no benefit to their career. I could understand this to be true for workers, but not for business leaders attending the seminar. My premise, expectation and anticipated responses were cross-culturally misplaced!

First Plant Visit

The tour of plants would at least satisfy my curiosity, allowing me to observe and learn about the Russian manufacturing industries I was permitted to visit. This was a city closed to foreigners, so I was certain there were restrictions limiting what I would see. The first visit taught me that the government controlled what was to be produced. The shoe manufacturing plant had a monthly quota of shoes to be fabricated.

I am sure the intention of visiting the shoe factory was to impress me. I drew this conclusion when I observed their conveyor belts were turned up to such a high rate of speed that they could have launched planes off an aircraft carrier. Surely, this was to indicate high productivity rates. However, there were no workers anywhere to place shoes on the conveyor belts! The second thing that amazed me was their explanation: there was a leather shortage so leather shoes were not being made.

However, in another part of the factory they were making cloth slippers. To my utter surprise, one pair of cloth slippers was counted as equivalent to one pair of leather shoes. As a result, they attained their monthly government shoe quota at that time by making cloth slippers. What an unusual way to achieve gross national output. It was likely many Russian consumers wanted leather shoes and were saving their rubles to purchase the shoes they needed – especially in a society that required a lot of walking to get around, since the majority of people were unable to own a car.

A Small Group Dinner

Dr. Kalmykov planned a dinner in the restaurant of my hotel to include my two translators, Victor and Michael. Walking through the hotel toward the restaurant, I passed the men's room that emitted an overpowering odor, which, fortunately did not permeate to the restaurant. The conversation among the four of us allowed us to become more socially acquainted. It also helped me learn about self-deprecating Russian humor. We were served a tasty-looking molded salad concoction that included green peas. Michael could not resist commenting. As he looked at our salad molded in the shape of a pyramid he said, "This restaurant serves seven different salads during a week: the same recipe, but it comes in seven different shapes, one for each day of the week."

This was our first formal dinner together. Typical Russian style, we were served very small glasses of vodka. After I finished the unpleasant drink, I was asked if I would like a second. I said, "No thank you, I really don't drink liquor." Immediately I was asked, "Well what is your fuel?" I said, "Pepsi Cola." "Well, well," said Vladimir Kalmykov, "we just happen to have the director of the Pepsi plant attending our seminars. Our plant visit is to his Pepsi plant tomorrow, and you shall never be without Pepsi." And this commitment became true.

A Workforce Problem

Several plant managers approached Dr. Kalmykov sometime during the first seminar week. They told him that plant visits were preferred for the mornings when the plants were better manned and productive. Why? Because of food shortages, the workers leave their factory jobs in the afternoons to stand in lines to buy food. Dr. Kalmykov was concerned about how strong the afternoon seminar attendance would be with the managers. He did not want to upset the very first seminar and take a chance to test it. In fact, he did not like the idea at all and dismissed it. I did not know about this until many months later. The morning seminars continued, which may have reduced the chance for my associates to see a variety of plants as hoped. And as a professor and educator, Dr. Kalmykov very likely placed more value on seminar class time for which the attendees paid, compared to factory visits not paid for and had poor turnouts because of poor interest.

Apparently workers were paid a fixed monthly sum regardless of hours worked. I even learned that Dr. Kalmykov's teaching load was only six hundred hours annually.

Seventeen

The second day seminar session went very well. Tuesday was a day of apprehension for both Dr. Kalmykov and me. I had tested him by asking for permission to bring Bibles into Russia to distribute in the seminar. He answered, "You may bring 'text books' into Russia." At the end of that morning's session, I told the audience I would bring in a textbook for them the next day. They could keep it or leave it for the students at the language Institute. I said the textbook is the Bible in the Russian language, that there are verses in the Bible that have application to many business principles and each seminar leader would use a Bible verse or verses that related to the subject he presented. Surprisingly, there were no reactions or comments as everyone left after the seminar session for the lunch break

Second Plant Visit

After lunch, nine seminar attendees again showed up for a Pepsi plant tour. Since Pepsi is a US beverage product, it appeared that the equipment probably was supplied by the parent company. We observed the clean bottles enter the Pepsi filling equipment. The filled bottles traveled in a single row past a back-lit opaque plastic panel that aided inspection of the fill level in the bottles. The continuous stream of bottles permitted comparison of the fill level with many adjacent bottles at a time. The fill heights varied widely up and down by two inches; a much poorer fill control than expected.

Farther down the Pepsi line, a mechanic was working on a new automated packaging machine. He was trying to overcome a difficulty with packing Pepsi bottles into cartons. Before our tour ended, we made a very brief visit to the other side of the Pepsi plant where wine was being bottled.

Imagine an enlarged bicycle chain with each link eight inches long and four inches wide. On the wine side of the plant, large conveyor chains traveled in many directions on the production floor. They were eighteen inches off the floor with sheet-metal safety guards mounted six inches away from both sides of the conveyor chain. No wooden steps existed to help workers cross over the chain conveyors. Several times I stepped over a moving chain that would look very hazardous to anyone not accustomed to manufacturing environments. Quite likely, it would have caused an American OSHA inspector to have a heart attack before he had time to write a safety violation citation! We spent less than fifteen minutes in this side of the plant.

The best outcome was that Dr. Kalmykov arranged for me to have a personal supply of Pepsi during my stay in Russia. He had learned very fast that Pepsi, not Vodka, was my fuel.

Eighteen

"Textbook" Distribution

I greeted Wednesday with a degree of apprehension. What would be the response to the Bibles? Concern was immediately dispelled when we arrived. The seminar attendees had lined up single file in the hallway like school children, waiting for the distribution of the Bibles. I never expected such a positive response. This day I presented the four factors of production that exist in any manufacturing endeavor. I had the class turn to Matthew 21:33-34, a parable Jesus taught of the vineyard.

> **"Listen to another parable: There was a landowner who planted a vineyard. He put a wall around it, dug a winepress in it and built a watchtower. Then he rented the vineyard to some farmers and went away on a journey. When the harvest time approached, he sent his servants to the tenants to collect his fruit."**

The four factors were: 1) *entrepreneur ability*, i.e., a businessman, 2.) *land* that was purchased, 3) *capital*, which was represented by investment in the wall, winepress and watch tower, and 4) *labor* that was hired to work and man the vineyard. It was a successful day to be able to relate the Bible and business together. No dialog ensued during or after this session.

News Spreads

With 60 people in the seminar, news spread about an American business-man leading a business seminar in Gorky. My afternoons became filled with schedules to meet with and sometimes speak to assembled employees in different entities, such as employees of a bank. The bank supposedly dated back to the House of Romanov (1613-1917). I explained how I had savings accounts and checking accounts in my local bank. What really surprised the people was our use of personal checking accounts in the U.S.

Moral Danger Included

A local young Russian entrepreneur was operating a business training program. I was told that he wished to engage in some sort of joint venture with Ziebell Associates. I had no interest but agreed to meet at his office. My translator Michael knew about this man. He warned me that he hired only Russian Beauty Queens as female employees. Michael was right. The man led us to a very low to the floor couch without legs. Next I observed at eye level pairs of beautifully-shaped legs below miniskirts walking back and forth in front of us, serving cookies and tea. The entrepreneur made overtures about wanting to establish a business alliance with my firm. I explained that providing business seminars was my only purpose in coming to Russia.

Then he insisted we come to a lunch the next day in the dining room of my hotel to celebrate my visit to the city. His seating arrangement placed a gorgeous blue-eyed brunette across from me and a pretty blond to my right between Michael and me. I was familiar with the saying, "The eyes are the window to the soul." The brunette's blue eyes turned seductive, conveying adulterous intent by staring piercingly into my own eyes, as if to gain a hold on my soul. God's Holy Spirit instantly warned me. Not all readers will believe this unless they have similarly experienced a temptress. I immediately cut her off by not making any eye contact with her for the duration of lunch. I was quite sure I had read her intensions correctly.

The First Escape

I was relieved when Michael spoke up about "another meeting" we had to attend right after lunch. When we left, I told him about the brunette's attempt. "Well," he said, "the blond was rubbing her leg up and down my leg!" There now was no doubt about the immoral method the man used to make business alliances or attract clients for his business training program.

Now, despite our recent experiences with the young entrepreneur, we felt we should honor the unfortunate previous commitment we had made to visit his off-site educational camp some miles into the countryside where his business sessions were held. We intentionally drove to the camp very late in the afternoon, determined not to stay long. There appeared to be a fair number of men enrolled in his program, and there was an abundant number of Beauty Queens on the property. Quite likely, the camp was not only for business training but perhaps a camp for "affordable companionship," which transgresses the Seventh Commandment and destroys men and marriages.

The Second Escape

We planned to arrive late enough to miss the camp dinner. The sun was beginning to set, and evening was imminent. The determined entrepreneur begged us to swing by and visit his dacha. In my mind, I sensed the potential for entrapment. All I could envision was walking up to the door of his dacha, having a Beauty Queen step out to greet us in a Victoria's Secret's outfit and then there would be the unheard click of a camera from behind a nearby tree. Any success with staged entrapment could lead to attempted blackmail. Michael quickly invented another excuse for leaving by explaining that we had "an obligation" for a very important late evening meeting. Surely, our host understood that many people like him wanted to meet with me. We departed gracefully and with haste. That ended my contact with this Russian "entrepreneur."

Nineteen

The seminar attendees had their Bibles overnight, but this morning very few brought them. Perhaps they did not want to be seen with a Bible in public or had decided not to take any risks by keeping it safe at home. However, there was one very upset gentleman talking with Dr. Kalmykov in the hallway. He was the director of the Pepsi plant but had been absent when the Bibles where distributed. He was very pleased when we had a Bible available to give to him.

Responses from a few of the people who received Bibles follow:

- The Director of Technology in a plastics plant said when his wife saw the Bible, she immediately started to cry. This was the first time she had seen a Bible, and she began reading it after dinner. The Director presented me with a tiny metal lapel pin, just like the one he awarded to plant employees who were recognized for good job performance.
- A woman economist said she had seen the Bible one time when she was 12 years old and never after that. Another female

economist had never seen the Bible in her life. Her enthusiastic words were, "And now we each have one to read!"

The Summer Camp

Directors of several plants in a food products conglomerate attended the seminar. They invited Michael and me to their countryside summer camp that was made available to their employees for summer vacations. They wanted us to be their guests for a special dinner.

Our country drive through one very small village led to a countryside road that was muddy, deeply rutted and better suited for army tanks and trucks to maneuver. The central camp building was next to a wide, deep, rock-strewn river with a good flowing current. It was a very cool day in the middle of August, and my bones were still cold. The gathering included seven older senior executives accompanied by a few wives and secretaries.

A Russian Sauna

The first order of activity for the men was a Russian sauna, something I had never experienced. Saunas are popular with Russians. Only "birthday suits" are worn for this event. We all picked a place to sit on a two-tier wooden bench. The top tier was the hottest place to sit. I chose the lower bench, where it was hot enough for me. It felt so good to absorb the heat into my body. After about 15 minutes, the chill in my bones still called for more time in the hot steam. One man splashed cups of water onto hot rocks to maintain the steam's temperature.

The men on the upper bench behind me were sweating and talking. They began to laugh. I asked Michael what was amusing them. He said they were surprised to learn that Americans do not sweat. I wasn't sweating, because I had not reached a temperature hot enough to warm my bones. But after another ten minutes, they learned Americans do sweat. They told me to lie down on my stomach and then began to beat my backside with willow branches, just as they did to one another. It really stings, but the purpose is to stimulate sweating. I can attest that the torture does work! Next, the Russians planned that we all would run outside and jump into the river. I expressed concern about the women being somewhere nearby, so my companions appeased me and agreed to jump into their indoor swimming pool a few steps from the sauna. The water in the pool was perfectly still, and the surface looked like a silver glass mirror. The sheen was from body oils floating on the water surface from sweating people plunging into the pool to cool off. The oils and water became well mixed after the first several Russians jumped into the pool.

After our Pool Plunge

As I dressed after the sauna, I looked in a mirror. My face was as red as a cooked lobster. My bones now felt warm again. I learned the sauna is an enjoyable bonding experience for Russians. I say "Russians" because I have seen photographs of Scandinavian men and women all sitting together in a steaming sauna. I was glad I was not exposed to that kind of experience.

A Banquet Surprise

Afterward, a very long table was set up with a lot of excellent food without any Pepsi available, I took tiny sips from my small glass of vodka, making it last in order to avoid another serving. The crowd was very jovial, when, oddly, the attention turned to me. Michael turned to me and said a question has been raised. One of the secretaries was inquiring if I was willing to have a photograph taken with us kissing. To go along with the jovial crowd, a middle-aged woman and I walked to the end of the banquet table and kissed for the camera. There was a lot of applause. I am sure that photograph brought her fame among her acquaintances as proof of kissing an American. When I returned to my home in the States, I told my wife about the kissing incident. As my ever-trusting wife, Jean had no concern over my confession.

The Kiss

Twenty

Day Five and Payback Time

On Friday I completed my seminar presentation. By this time, the attendees were participating with questions and comments; I hoped that would continue with the other seminar leaders who would come. Dr. Kalmykov had the names of all those enrolled in the seminar. He handed out Certificates of Completion from this seminar that was sponsored by his organization, Polyglott. The recipients appeared to be pleased with the seminar and were looking forward to the next one that would follow soon.

Victor translated for me that last seminar day, after which Dr. Kalmykov took us to a fried chicken lunch at a small restaurant overlooking the Volga River. We watched the river traffic as we ate and talked. I was fascinated by the Russian boats that traveled quite fast on underwater hydrofoils (skis) that lifted the hull of the boat completely above the river surface. Travel by river has been important throughout Russia's history. Even now, the Volga River and all its tributaries provide travel for the east-to-west and north-to-south Russian landmass that spreads across two time zones, spanning a width of eight hundred miles east of Moscow.

Payback Time

Because the Language Institute had accommodated the seminar, it was now payback time with an event for the students. An afternoon auditorium assembly was planned for all the language students. I was asked to speak to the students and then answer questions they had written out in English and submitted on small pieces of paper. There were easily 300 students in the audience. I assumed the administration would have screened and selected the questions I received.

The first question surprised me. I was asked if I considered myself romantic. I was always moved by romantic movies and novels, so my reply was that yes, I did consider myself romantic. Afterward, I second-guessed my answer, because "romantic" could be considered from different viewpoints. I hoped the students had not misinterpreted my response to mean loose sexually. As evidenced to me several times, some Russians held a quite liberal viewpoint, and the B class American movies they view in their theaters do not convey good moral standards.

Interest in U.S. Life

The second question was amusing and revealed how U.S. culture can appear to foreigners. The student wrote, "I saw an American bank robbery movie. Everyone fell to the floor when the shooting began. Are people trained to do this in the U.S.?" How would you as the reader of this book answer this question?

A sampling of questions from students follows In English <u>just</u> as they were written:

- How many cars do you have?
- What time do you begin and end your workday?
- Do you have recreational activities?
- How long are your vacations and where do you go?
- What number of hours per day do wives spend shopping?
- What is your wife's daily routine
- Tell us about the production of automobiles.
- How does Christianity help you?
- You've said the America is watching the Soviets. Do not you understand you will see nothing (nothing good) till the communists guard the Russia. It is like 2+2. What do you think about that?
- You have certainly met people who ran the country and boss the industry. Do you think they correspond the task that faces them, that they are capable of improving the situation here?

One Social Evening

There was a third translator available who did not translate for me on this trip. He and his wife had just been granted permission to realize their dream: to occupy a two-bedroom apartment of their own. They beamed with pride as I arrived as their American guest. A neighbor couple plus Michael and I made six altogether. We sat on stuffed furniture around a living room coffee table and ate together.

Later, I made a cross-cultural mistake – one that I will never make again. After many other questions, the wife of the new apartment owners asked me to describe my house: four bedrooms and two baths upstairs, living room, dining room, family room, kitchen, a den, powder room and utility room on the ground floor, as well as a finished basement and office. I never will forget what the wife said; "Well, now I am not so happy with my apartment." It was a terrible response for me to hear. I was not trying to impress my hosts, but I am prone to answer a question without assessing the situation. I felt badly for not being more discerning with my answer.

The Literacy Test

Within minutes, I demonstrated my lack of literacy. From my observations, the average educated Russian is likely to display a collection of books behind glass shelves or in book cabinets in his living room. Russia as a nation is a little above average in reading literacy. This couple had books by Mark Twain. They asked, "Is it true Americans are not allowed to read Mark Twain's books?" I said no, that his works are widely read. One of the Russians said, "See, I thought that was propaganda!"

Then the kicker question came; "Have you read works by American author Theodore Dreiser?" I replied, "No, I have not." They had read a lot of his writings. I did not know who he was, and I don't think I admitted not knowing of him. The first question I asked my wife within 15 minutes of arriving home from Russia was, "Have you ever heard of the American author Theodore Dreiser?" She hadn't. We quickly pulled out our tattered bound high school book *The Literature of the United States – An anthology and a history* copyright, 1949. Only one of his stories, *The Second Choice,* appeared on pages 998-1008.

The Soviet Union favored his portrayals about the U.S. during the terrible hardship of our tragic 1930s dust bowl years. Dreiser (1871-1945) was a leftist in thought, labeled barbaric, later to become registered as a communist near the end of his life. The Communist leadership used his writings to portray a poor image of America to the Russians when the USSR suffered famine and starvation in their own country under Stalin.

Much of USSR's suffering was caused by the communist reorganization of their agriculture into state-run collective farms, thus resulting in loss of individual incentive toward productivity. I visited a rural village in a Russian collective farming district. Upon walking onto a field that had been "harvested" of carrots, I saw amazing quantities of carrots lying on the top soil. I could not guess the percentage of unharvested carrot crop left as spoilage

Twenty-One

VOLGA RIVER BOAT TRIP

On Saturday, we welcomed the opportunity for an adventure: a trip down the Volga River on a 125-foot-long power boat to the riverside Makaryev Monastery, founded in 1415 by the missionary Saint Macarius. Our group included Dr. Kalmykov and me, six other men and three women. Our accommodation was a small stateroom below deck for the downriver half of our round trip. I did not realize one man in our group was a newspaper reporter. It may have been Dr. Kalmykov's plan for publicity for his Polyglott business seminars. By this time, the seminar had already begun to receive newspaper coverage. I have copies of many published articles that appeared in Russian newspapers covering the entire year-long seminar program.

My traveling companions – both the men and the women - took turns asking me questions about my family, employment, impressions of the Russian people and Russia, as well as questions about the United States. Two things particularly impressed me: the women's mainly positive responses to my answers, and the reporter's mostly negative reactions. He obviously assumed I spoke propaganda about myself and the United States, and his demeanor and verbal responses were rude. I decided the reporter must be so steeped in cold war propaganda and counter-propaganda that there was very little chance he could hear or discern truth. Or perhaps what I described was so very different from his life experience it was like describing Disney World to someone with no reference point to which he could make comparisons.

The Monastery

While the Q&A session may have lasted a little over an hour, it felt like three hours with the presence of the oppressive newspaper reporter. It was a relief when it was announced that Makaryev had come into view. We went topside and enjoyed the sunshine and fresh air. A massive, thick, 650-foot-long, white wall stood as a fortress with huge, stout, round defense towers at three of the four corners, providing protection for the monastery buildings and grounds in ancient times. It was an impressive site of historic fame.

In 1439, the original monastery was burned by Tatar Khan Ulu Mukhammed. He captured Macarius, the original builder, and held him captive, releasing him only after his prisoner promised he would not rebuild the monastery. Much later, in 1620, Monk Avramy (Abraham), along with many more monks, began work on the first wooden Cathedral of the Holy Trinity, completing it in 1642. More stone monastery buildings were added from 1651 to 1667. The massive stone walls present today date from that era and stand as a tribute to unimaginable amounts of human labor. When I stood in the cavernous, vaulted, masonry rooms inside the Makaryev Monastery buildings, I felt very small. Looking down at the Volga River from arched porticos, I observed a number of fishermen in long row boats trying to catch czar fish, which I already had experienced to be very bony and greasy.

Site of Historic Commerce

The annual Makaryev Fair took place every summer for two centuries outside the monastery walls and was one of the most important and famous merchant fairs in Eastern Europe. From the 1620s, it was an important event in the Russian economy. By 1800, more than 3,000 government and private buildings housed millions of rubles worth of trade goods. Imagine what that ancient scene must have looked like with the crowds of both men and women, wearing regional traditional clothing, showing their trade goods and haggling with one another. Amidst their shouting and the laughter of children running about, the smoke and odors of cooking over camp fires would have hung over them.

A court physician, G. Rehmann, attending the 1805 Makaryev Fair viewed countless stalls skirting the walls of the Makaryev Monastery. Merchants were selling everything from Persian carpets and Kashmir shawls to Siberian furs. He was fascinated by a long row of carts bearing wooden vessels for everyday use; [1] hand painted bowls, dishes and sundry items widely known today as Khokhloma (huck'-la-ma) which originated in the Nizhny Novgorod region in the 1600s. At the present time Khokhloma continues to be a huge industry with an international marketing reach.

In 1816, a massive fire at Makaryev destroyed most of the merchants' buildings and extensive inventory and, thus, most of their wealth. So,

1 Leningrad, Russia, Aurora Art Publishers, 1980, *Khokhloma Folk Painting*, 10.

in 1817, the fair moved to Nizhny Novgorod and now, once again is famous.[2]

Return to Nizhny Novgorod

We boarded our boat and headed back up river, thankful for the excursion and the visit to Makaryev. Again I was awed every time one of the Russian hydrofoil power boats passed us with its entire hull raised a couple of feet above the river surface. I admired the Russians for their fleets of these unique boats used for public mass transit.[2]

2 Makaryev Monastery, http://en.wikipedia.org/wiki/Markaryev_Monastery (accessed October 19, 2015).

Twenty-Two

During my first week in Nizhny Novgorod, I had asked Dr. Vladimir Kalmykov if there was a Protestant church in the city. He is Russian Orthodox, but he thought there was such a church nearby. His inquiry resulted in a visit to my hotel room by him and three men from the church. I must have passed their interview, because they invited me to come to their church's Sunday morning service and to be prepared to greet their congregation.

My First Visit to the Baptist Church

The church was located in an old neighborhood with very similar one-story, wood-sided homes. One of the homes had been converted into the Baptist Church. The house was painted green and was surrounded on both sides and the back of the property by a green wooden wall about seven feet tall.

Where 1990 -92 House Church Services were held

Vladimir and I

On Sunday morning, we entered a wooden gate and walked into the back yard where many men, women and children were mingling. Vladimir explained I was the American who had come to meet their pastor. A man went into the church and returned in a couple minutes and invited us into a room where six men were seated. After we were seated, the small room was packed. The deacons prayed for the pastor before their church service began.

Pastor Vasily

Pastor Vasily Semyonov was an elderly man with a gray beard and glasses. We were introduced to the clergyman and I told him I was bringing greetings to their congregation from my congregation in the United States. I gave the pastor a Christian book in Russian titled *New Testament Documents*. The deacons and a couple of choir members greeted me. Two deacons again led in prayer, the pastor read Scripture and then prayed before we entered the packed church.

I sat on a small raised platform with the pastor and deacons. The platform was against a wall with a short, stout wooden railing on both sides and the front of the platform. Simple wooden benches packed with families sitting shoulder-to-shoulder filled the space around the platform. There was a small balcony against the far wall, nine feet above the main floor. Three rows of benches packed with people sitting shoulder-to-shoulder were behind the railing panel.

Pastor Vasily stood up and informed the congregation that "an American Christian has come to extend a greeting from his American church to our congregation." As he nodded, I stood, Vladimir translated, and I greeted the people in the name of Jesus Christ, stating that the members of my church send their greeting to their congregation. I told them I was the first deputy (Russian organizational terminology) in Slavic Gospel Association and explained I was leading business seminars in Nizhny Novgorod. When I thanked the people for allowing me to greet them, everyone stood up and silently showed their appreciation with a slight bow from the waist, then sat down and the worship service continued.

Pastor Vasily and the Author

A Lunch Invitation

The worship service lasted two hours. Dr. Kalmykov and I were invited to stay for a lunch that was prepared and served in the basement. We accepted the invitation. Many pastors and deacons across the land had spent some time in prison during past communist persecution of Christians. As a result, it is beyond their experience to have someone from outside of Russia show up at their church, especially in their city closed to foreigners. I expected I would be "vetted," since they would want to be sure I was the Christian I claimed to be and not a potential risk to them.

In the basement, there were two 25-foot-long tables with chairs on all sides. One table was for the men. I sat at one end; Pastor Vasily sat at the far end facing me. The deacons and male leaders sat along the sides. A prayer of blessing was said for the food, and the women began serving borscht, rice and watermelon, bread and tea. Then all the women sat at the other table to eat and listen to my answers to the "vetting" questions.

Vladimir translated as the pastor asked me to speak about my family and mission. I told them about my family, about the SGA mission started by a Russian who migrated to the United States and had a burden for the Russian people to hear the gospel. As we ate, I gave them my personal testimony about coming to Christ at age 24 and my study of the Bible to better understand the Scriptures, including baptism, communion and church doctrine. I mentioned the possibility of having a sister church relationship with my home church, and they expressed interest. They were building a new church on a nearby piece of land.

After some announcements, Pastor Vasily asked me to present a sermon the following Sunday. Vladimir and I left the gathering after having enjoyed the very good Russian borscht and prepared foods and a lengthy conversation. My Russian companion had never participated in a discussion like the one he had just experienced. He said he was very amazed by Vasily's sermon and teaching.

Because Vladimir was a language professor, I was not surprised when he said, "The manner in which Vasily spoke showed that he is not highly schooled, but still very interesting with his preaching." It is well known that communism suppressed education for Protestants, in addition to persecuting many Christians. Vladimir's critique interested me; it revealed observable evidence of the effects wrought by communism upon the life of people like Pastor Vasily because of the deprivation of education.

Twenty-Three

At Pastor Vasily's request, I prepared a 20-minute sermon for Sunday's church service. I selected two passages in the New Testament that contain some of the basic teaching and encouragement that bind together all Christians around the world:

1 Peter 1: 13-19

Therefore, prepare your minds for action; be self-controlled; set your hope fully on the grace to be given you when Jesus Christ is revealed. As obedient children, do not conform to the evil desires you had when you lived in ignorance. But just as he who called you is holy, so be holy in all you do; for it is written: "Be holy, because I am holy." Since you call on a Father who judges each man's work impartially, live your lives as strangers here in reverent fear. For you know that it was not with perishable things such as silver or gold that you were redeemed from the empty way of life handed down to you from your forefathers, but with the precious blood of Christ, a lamb without blemish or defect. NIV

1 John 4:1-6

Dear friends, do not believe every spirit, but test the spirits to see whether they are from God, because many false prophets have gone out into the world. This is how you can recognize the Spirit of God: Every spirit that acknowledges that Jesus Christ has come in the flesh is from God, but every spirit that does not acknowledge Jesus is not from God. This is the spirit of the antichrist, which you have heard is coming and even now is already in the world. You, dear children, are from God and have overcome them, because the one who is in you is greater than the one who is in the world. They are from the world and therefore speak from the viewpoint of the world, and the world listens to them. We are from God, and whoever knows God listens to us; but whoever is not from God does not listen to us. This is how we recognize the Spirit of truth and the spirit of falsehood. NIV

A young woman, Tamara, from their choir who was fluent in English, translated my sermon. She was a former student at the language institute where Dr. Kalmykov teaches. I noticed, as I spoke, some people in the balcony and on the main floor wiped tears from their eyes. I believe their response was not only because I was the first American they had seen, but also I was a Christian and spoke about our shared belief in Jesus Christ. I was also an unexpected visitor breaking through years of the old cold war barrier between our countries with biblical truths – truths that bound American and Russian Christians together despite former distortions by communist propaganda and international politics that had separated us.

The Service Included Communion

Two beautiful large round loaves of home-baked bread and six large goblets of wine stood on a table in the center of the platform. Pastor Vasily and the deacons wiped their hands with a damp cloth before breaking the bread, and the pastor asked me to say a word about Communion. The deacons then broke the loaves of bread; I removed a piece with them, after which the half loaves were given to the congregation. As a loaf was passed, each person removed a piece of bread, prayed silently, ate the bread and paused prayerfully before sitting down.

Again, the pastor asked me to read a portion of Scripture concerning the wine. The goblets contained a dark red, sweet wine. As the congregation stood, the goblets were passed as common cups from worshiper to worshiper. Each worshiper stood and received a goblet, took a sip of wine and passed the goblet to the next person. After each person sipped the wine, he continued to stand, prayed and then sat down. This was the first time I experienced the passing of a common wine goblet. I was greatly relieved I had taken a sip of the wine from a goblet after only six deacons had sipped from it, rather than having to participate from a goblet passed through a large crowd of people.

Second Basement Lunch

Dr. Kalmykov and I stayed for lunch. The seating arrangement was just as it had been the previous Sunday.

After lunch, we traveled to the construction site where the concrete foundation for their new church recently had been poured. During the construction, some women had served as laborers, and many of the women had prepared meals at the site for the workers. A very fine-looking brick service building had been built to safeguard tools and building supplies. The attractively-designed 1,000-seat church was expected to take three years to complete using volunteer labor.

I was invited back for a 2:00 p.m. repeat of the morning service held for people who traveled from farther out in the countryside. The service again lasted two hours. Before the service, I gave Pastor Vasily a new *Goetze Russian Bible*. He held it like a prized possession and asked me to write in it and autograph it to show it was intended to be a gift to him personally. I learned that, otherwise, it would be considered a gift to the church.

The Church in Action

Despite years of former communist persecution, the Gorky Baptist Church now had an out-reach ministry. On some Sundays, a bus would take leaders and choir members to evangelistic services in other cities that did not have a protestant church. They also had started a children's Sunday school twenty-one miles away in a city named Dzerzhinsk that did not have a Protestant church. Noteworthy is the fact that this city bears the name of Felix Dzerzhinsky, the founder of the communist secret police and Director (1917-1926) of the KGB. [1]

During the Gorky church construction period from 1990 to 1993, Christian literature, Bibles and Children Picture Bibles were in great demand by the people in Nizhny Novgorod and beyond. The quantities of literature Slavic Gospel Association provided to the church helped them raise funds to purchase building materials. While the church's construction of the superstructure was underway, two accidents occurred: a 62-year-old woman fell from a wall and was killed, and a man fell and shattered both legs. A photograph of the church is a monumental testimony to the thousands of labor hours expended to build the very impressive-looking church.

With the balcony it could hold 1000 worshipers

---

1 Felix Dzerzhinsky, https://en.wikipedia.org/wiki/Felix_Dzerzhinsky, (accessed: December 28, 2016).

Twenty-Four

Last Week of Whirlwind Activity

I t was very satisfying to be invited to speak to a great variety of business leaders and employees, at research institutes, to a student body and other organizations. The intensity of this activity sometimes brought me close to physical exhaustion. My host and translators were anxious for me to be seen as much as possible in and around Nizhny Novgorod. Most likely two driving forces were behind this activity: they were enjoying being seen hosting an American, and others I met were able to tell friends about spending time with an American. I know the same motivation tends to exist in every culture when hosting a visiting foreigner.

But remember, these inside Russia observations, events and circumstances in 1990 – now almost thirty years ago – are dated as I write about them now, in 2017. Big changes were just beginning to happen in Russia under Gorbachev. Present day Russia has undergone many changes during the interim: but not all are positive.

Product Development

I was taken to meet with a small product development team. My translator and I sat around a small table with three Russian engineers. They were anxious to tell me about a security alarm they were developing for automobiles. Russia's supply of automobiles was limited. Most citizens could not afford to buy a car, which probably greatly contributed to car thefts. One observable example illustrates responses to the shortage of auto windshield wipers. Whether it was raining or not, after parking his car, the driver removed the wiper blades and locked them in the car to keep them from being stolen, or the wipers were kept in the car and not mounted until it began to rain.

Victor was the only one of the five translators who owned a car, and his high-rise apartment building was built by the government without garages. He rented a single-car garage a mile away from his apartment. He had a padlock on the door of the garage as it was too far away for personal surveillance. Even with locks, some car owners found their garages broken into and their cars missing.

The car alarm developers explained how the device worked to help prevent car thefts. I asked them what selling price they were considering. I was surprised when they did not have one in mind! They were not using any criteria for a cost goal or selling price. My U.S. product development experience always contained cost and selling price targets. I left this meeting genuinely dismayed by the lack of market planning in product development efforts. Later I realized Russian car owners probably would pay any price for a device that would prevent their car from being stolen. Still, a car alarm making a sound a mile away from the owner's apartment would be a problem, particularly if nearby residents ignored the sound. Because the government determined market selling prices, it would have been interesting to know how they determined the final pricing on anything.

The City Wharf on the Volga River

The volume of boat traffic fascinated me. Down at the Nizhny, Volga River wharf, boats regularly arrived and docked. Crowds of people would disembark loaded with mostly produce to sell. One man carried more ripe purple grapes than I thought anyone could possibly carry. He had customers buying from him before he had time to leave the wharf. Crowds of people were boarding the boats for other destinations or for the return trip home somewhere along the Volga River. It was a very different lifestyle to witness.

Under Communism, both boat and air fares had been kept very low so people living even 1,000 miles or more away from Moscow or other big cities were provided low cost travel to enable them to participate in commerce. As an example, a farmer could pack up as many pounds of tomatoes and produce that could be hand carried, fly to Moscow, sell the produce on the street, fly back home a thousand miles and make a profit.

Dacha Visit

Translator Victor taught at the Inland Waterways Academy. He seemed financially better off than others translating for Dr. Kalmykov's Polyglott organization. In addition to owning a car, he had property out in the countryside where he personally built a dacha. He wanted me to spend a day visiting him there.

I was very surprised and impressed. With supposedly limited availability of building materials, Victor had managed to build a small two-story house with three bedrooms upstairs. The first floor had a small living room next to a kitchen-eating room. An outhouse stood on the back property line next to a larger structure that was a sauna he had built. The fenced property had a cultivated variety of fruit trees, a vegetable garden and raspberry bushes, all well tilled and carefully maintained.

One of Victor's greatest challenges had been finding a scrap iron stove for the sauna. He had accomplished all this in a country that considers everything including scrap wood boards as property of the State. So, while it was the former Communist Letter of the Law to claim all forms of resources as State property, it seemed otherwise in this dacha community, where the people apparently lived by the code, "Get whatever you can get when you can find it." I found his dacha to be a self-created piece of Eden that gave Victor and his family a wonderful countryside retreat miles away from their high-rise, government-built apartment building in Nizhny Novgorod.

An Evening of Hospitality

Michael Dashkov received an invitation for us to visit a woman and some of her neighbors in her apartment. We arrived at about 7:00 p.m to find there were a man and three women present, and I soon realized I was the focus of the gathering. Everyone wanted to get some understanding about life in America and to hear my impressions of my two-and-a-half weeks in Nizhny Novgorod. I told them about the U.S. and my life. Their inability to comprehend a U.S. supermarket was understandable, given what I had seen in their city. My evening of conversation and exchanges with our host and her neighbors was very lively and engaging.

The Russians probed about my Christian faith and practice and found it very interesting and compared it to Russian Orthodoxy. They were elated when I gave them some Christian books and a Bible written in Russian. It was very satisfying to witness the positive reception they gave to these gifts and to my visit. All the Russians I met excelled in their hospitality.

The host provided some hot tea and cookies during the evening. Frequently the people sang songs together. They were disappointed when, at around 9:30 p.m., we indicated we had to leave. Our hostess had a telephone in her apartment – very unusual, since most people did not have one – so Mike called for a taxi and gave the address of the apartment. The cab did not arrive, so Mike called again at 10 o'clock and this time was told to go outside and wave down a cab himself. We decided to walk.

It was dark, and the street was totally deserted when we left the apartment and began a ten-block walk through a central residential part of the city back to my hotel. We saw only two people on our way. Mike said it was because a very popular TV program was on at that time. Very controversial people are interviewed, and a lot of music is included in the program. Mike suggested everyone was inside watching the program. I decided that included the cab drivers. It was said sometimes people order a cab three days in advance.

A Barbecue in the Forest

I never figured out why I was invited to this event. There were six couples and Mike and I. It was a long way to get to our destination located in an isolated birch tree forest somewhere in the Russian nation. The grill was going with unappetizing small cuts of pork heavy with fat.

I don't remember participating in any memorable verbal interaction with the men. Everyone was drinking vodka. The only significant memory I have is that the women all stayed close together twenty feet away, drank a lot of vodka and laughed a lot. But what astounded me was what the women did after they swallowed the vodka. They had jars of homemade dill pickle preserves, and they used the juice from the pickles for chasers. I could hardly believe it. It gave testimony to how terrible vodka tastes. Vodka and dill pickle juice together seemed unpalatable to me. I wondered how one's stomach could even digest such a mixture!

It was a struggle, but I did manage to eat a few pieces of the cooked pork. When it was time to leave the forest, I was very glad to depart.

Perhaps the whole event was meant to show me that even Russians know how to enjoy a barbecue in a beautiful forest setting.

Russian Icebreaker

I felt as though my bones were still chilled, in spite of all my activity. Victor had a solution; he arranged for us, through the Inland Waterway Academy, something he did not reveal to me. He escorted me to a brand-new Russian icebreaker on the Volga River. They name these ships after captains. This one was named after a Kapitan Zarubin. It was a sturdy steel ship freshly painted and attended by the captain and crew. This was the third week of August and well ahead of the time when the vessel would have to be icebreaking.

I was welcomed on board and taken down below to the wonderful sight of a sauna. I had it all to myself. It did a magnificent job of warming all the bones in my body. After I emerged from the sauna and dressed, I was given a full tour of the ship and the captain's wheelhouse with its 180 ° bow view of the river. Many brass gauges and instruments filled the back wall of the wheelhouse.

Afterward, I was served hot tea and visited with the captain and a couple crew members before we left the ship. It is very possible that was the very last time I would have a sauna on a Russian icebreaker, or for that matter on an icebreaker anywhere else in the world.

The Choir Director's Father

The choir director for the Gorky Baptist Church was a young man in his middle 20s. He insisted that Michael Dashkov and I come to his parents' home outside the city to have dinner and meet them and his sister.

Michael Dashkov and I approached their apartment in a two-story building. The outdoor scene attracted my artist's eye. A 15-foot-high red brick wall extended from the corner of the building. The wall contained an archway about 10 feet wide and 10 feet tall. To the right of the arch the remaining brick wall extended to the vertical broken jagged edge where the rest of the wall that had been destroyed. There was an overgrowth of brush and trees that gave it the appearance of neglect. The remaining picturesque wall and arch extending ninety degrees from the corner of the apartment building hinted that a very nice courtyard had once existed. When I returned home, I oil painted a picture of how I imagined the courtyard might have looked. On a later trip back to Russia I gave the painting shown below to the family.

Upon entering the apartment, we were greeted by the young director's father, mother and sister, all of whom expressed pleasure by our visit. A dinner table was nicely set, and we sat down to a delicious meal of potatoes, meat and vegetable, bread and tea. The family conversation turned toward the father with some laughter and kidding about his library. This was a devout Baptist family. The father was a man who eagerly sought Christian books wherever and from whomever he could borrow them. The family asked the father to bring out some of his library and show it to me.

It was both sad and inspiring at the same time. He brought out possibly 20 black and white composition books similar to those still used by school children in the U.S. During the reign of communism, the father would secretly locate, borrow and hand copy the entire content of a Christian book into a composition book or two. Over time, he built a massive personal library with these composition books that now stood in stacks from floor to ceiling. I could hardly believe the man had the endurance to build a private library of this size by hand copying so many books. The many, many hours it had taken to copy such a library were evidence of the thirst for Christian literature the father had during the worst years of communist religious oppression.

A Political Prisoner

Gorky (now Nizhny Novgorod) was closed to foreigners, because it was a major military armament and equipment manufacturing city during World War II. Its restrictive access enabled it to be used as an exile city where Russia's political prisoners were held by the Communist State. This usually included isolation from family and acquaintances. Local industries now include automotive, shipbuilding, and manufacturing of diesel engines, aircraft and machine tools.

I was driven to an apartment building in Nizhny Novgorod. My guide pointed to a first-floor apartment door and said, "That was the apartment of Russian Andre' Sakharov, a Soviet chief nuclear weapons scientist who was called 'father of the Soviet hydrogen bomb.' He was kept here for six years under house arrest for human rights protests. A 24-hour surveillance on him was maintained; any time he went out, a KGB agent followed him. He was released as late as December 23, 1986." [1]

As a champion of human rights and freedoms, Sakharov was an outspoken dissident to the Soviet regime and won the Nobel Peace Prize in 1975. Soviet authorities denied him permission to go to Norway to receive his award. On December 14, 1989, he made a plea before the Soviet Congress for political pluralism and a market economy. That very evening his wife and fellow dissident, Elena Bonner, found him dead in his library of a "heart attack."

The Artist

Dr. Kalmykov had a friend who was an artist. Knowing I liked to paint, he took me to his friend's studio. (my web site is – YurArt.com) I was astonished by the huge amount of floor space this artist had on a third story of an old building within a residential neighborhood. He had paintings leaning against one another with stacks lining the baseboard around all the walls of a room 60 ft by 40 ft., enough space for a dance studio.

I started thumbing through well over 100 paintings. Asked if I would be interested in buying one of them, I indicated that I would, if one interested me. Soon there were two paintings that interested me. One 16" x 20" on a canvas board was a very dark scene looking at the back of a horse-drawn wagon full of hay headed towards the distant barn just as the sun was disappearing over the horizon with a clear blue gray sky.

---

1 Phillip Taubman, "Sakharov Returns from Exile," <u>New York Times</u>, 24 December 1986, 1.

The brushstrokes were bold, and the painting spoke about the agrarian history of Russia that probably still existed in some areas.

The second painting, a 23" x 31" oil painting on stretched canvas, had a scene of Nizhny Novgorod in years past viewed from the north bank of the Oka River. It shows a lot of trees and foliage shading four buildings, including a four-story, reddish brick factory on the hillside. Three white Orthodox churches stand on the rising hill above the houses and factory. The artist's composition followed "artistic license." The viewer sees the Oka River just before it flows into the Volga River. White churches reflect off the surface of a back-water pool below the walkway and through the openings in a black wrought iron fence along a pedestrian walkway.

I purchased both paintings. Several days later a Lufthansa stewardess safely stored the wrapped paintings behind the last row of seats against a solid bulkhead for my flight home.

Epilogue

The business seminar program in Gorky utilized over a dozen of my American acquaintances to present seminar topics in Russia on their career specializations. After they return home, they provided a total of 427 pages of single spaced trip reports about their experiences and observations on five topics I had requested. This information became original research information that I used, along with my own experiences, to write my doctoral dissertation focused on cross-cultural business management. Copies of my dissertation are in the libraries of thirty-one U.S. universities and seminaries. Union Institute University selected my dissertation as one of the several research models for their new doctoral candidates to consider for their dissertation research methodology. Seminar leader George Layborne and his wife, Gail, plus my wife, Jean, attended my Doctoral graduation in 1992.

As you have read the many details of my personal experience in Gorky, it is fitting to add some of the different events and experiences other men had and how Russia impacted them. A few examples follow.

David Ingraham was an expert on small manufacturing businesses. He liked wearing loafers without socks. When he arrived in Russia, this did not go without notice by the Russians. When the Russians had a shortage of any item in their stores, the outage was called a "deficit."

Upon David's arrival, it was assumed that America had a deficit of socks, and this American had been unable to buy them. David had to assure the Russians that the U.S. had an abundant supply of socks. **Ed McCarthy** presented his seminar on marketing. After finishing his seminar week, he traveled on the night train back to Moscow. Upon awaking in the morning, he discovered his socks were missing.

On an anniversary of the famous Chernobyl Nuclear Reactor disaster, David was interviewed on TV. The interviewer tried to solicit negative comments from him. He instead maintained that nuclear power was a good alternative fuel source

American seminar speakers wearing button down collar shirts caused some Russians to go wild about the shirt style. Button downs became the desired new look, and several seminar leaders took in a fair number of button down shirts as gifts.

Once, **Pastor Vasily Semyonov** gave us very clear directions to his house in a small village. "After the last right-hand turn onto the last road, continue straight ahead until you will see a white goat tethered in the road and eating weeds. To the left of the goat is my house." We could not miss it.

Jim Harshaw worked in the finance department in hospitals and health care organizations. His seminar topic was business accounting. He included numerous checks and balances to prove accuracy and honesty in financial reporting. One day a Russian asked, "Well how do you cheat?" Taken aback for a minute, Jim responded, "Well, you make one number larger and another number smaller." The seminar broke into laughter.

A cab driver learned that Jim was an American, so he asked how Jim liked Nizhny Novgorod. During the cold war, the Russians had realized cities with large populations made better targets for atomic bombs. Jim said, "Before coming here, I wondered about the size of your city. I looked in an atlas and learned Nizhny Novgorod has a population of three million." The driver shot back, "I knew the government was lying! We were told our population was one million."

Because of Jim's hospital background, a visit was arranged to the city's 1000-bed children's hospital. While visiting the children's cancer ward, he learned that a shortage of cancer medicines existed, and the children's dosages were half of what they should receive. Additionally, the water used in the treatments contained pyrogens, fever producing substances, from not being highly purified.

This discovery greatly disturbed Jim. Upon returning home, Jim started an U.S. 501c3 non-profit organization named Plesion International. Nine men signed onto the Board of Directors. They immediately gathered used hospital equipment, received large donations of medicines and other hospital supplies and shipped numbers of full overseas containers to the children's hospital in Nizhny Novgorod. Within a year, Plesion's talented directors designed, built, shipped and installed a water purification system in the hospital.

Russia's critical shortages of hospital equipment and medical supplies remained without an end in sight. Months later, administrations in other city hospitals learned about Plesion's helping the children's hospital and reacted with jealousy. The post-communist city medical bureaucracy got involved and messed things up by holding and delaying containers delivered to Baltic shipyards. Container inspections began as political issues, and problems escalated, causing insurmountable difficulties. Plesion decided to move on and supply water purification systems to Romania, Africa and Viet Nam. At the time of this writing, Plesion International is a twenty-five-year-old humanitarian service organization.

Dr. Richard Baldwin taught international business as a professor at a well-established Christian College in Ohio. In Russia, he had his first experience being among people smoking and drinking vodka, a lifestyle that was the polar opposite of his college campus lifestyle. Secondly, he learned the Russians were unique in their willingness to engage in conversations about faith and a Christian testimony about biblical beliefs. He was struck by the observation: that there was more freedom to talk about the Bible, God and Jesus Christ, and that praying was much more open in Russia than it was in U.S. society outside of his Ohio campus. He realized his life on the campus now seemed sterile –, even a closed society. He had lost the feeling of interacting with people outside the Christian campus. It was an occasion of self-discovery. He resolved to have more off-campus interactions with an outreach to people who did not profess Christianity and to socialize with people who haven't heard that God loves them, even in spite of their resistance to love Him. Before leaving Russia, Dr. Baldwin witnessed one of Russia's first public democratic balloting processes. His host cast his ballot against keeping the Union of Republic States.

Another seminar leader reported he was looking away when his host slipped three papers into his hands to sign. He saw they were Soviet invitations for three men to come to the U.S. He did not know the men and refused to sign them. The host shrugged without a word. Later he learned that the person doing the inviting would have been responsible for their visitors' expenses in the U.S. and any necessary medical expenses.

Several of the later seminar speakers found themselves confronted by the same temptation from the **Beauty Queens** employed by the Advanced Management Institute. When my associates were invited by that institute's director to speak to an assembly of institute attendees, they also were confronted by the tactic I wrote about in Chapter 18. All the my seminar speakers successfully perceived the trap, evaded it and escaped. Because all these temptations planned by the Russian businessman failed, he exploded. He started an attack on Dr. Kalmykov's "Polyglot Cooperative" for its involvement with Christians – evidence of what can happen when a moral lifestyle collides with and rejects immoral enticements. In addition, under communism, it was a Russian societal norm to believe Christians were less educated and less intelligent people. The U.S. seminar leaders proved that stereotypical perception was wrong.

John Warton, the senior pastor of my church, volunteered to lead a seminar week on the topic of ethics. He was provided housing in a Russian hotel built ten years earlier. There was not one phone in the hotel. It was a cold February, and ten people stood in line to use a phone booth outside of the hotel.

John was interviewed about his seminar topic on ethics and was being filmed for a program to be advertised for a TV audience reported to be five million. During the filming, he was confronted with the view of "inequality of wealth as the illness of capitalism." John tactfully challenged his viewers by saying, "It is important to be just, to be profitable as much as you can while obeying the laws and help establish multiple sources to keep prices lower through competition."

Author with Pastors Vasily and John Warton

Pastor Vasily invited John to provide evangelistic encouragement to the crowd in Sputnik Auditorium in the communist named city of Dzerzhinsk. The place filled with an estimated turnout of over a thousand people. His words focused on Jesus' teachings and God's promises to faithful believers. Many in the audience came forward to express their faith in Jesus Christ.

Pastor John Warton & translator Tamara
Dzerzhinsk Newspaper Photo taken at Sputnik Auditorium service

A few years later **John Warton** established an organization that would assist entrepreneurs in many countries establish and expand their own business. The goal was to identify capable men and women and enable them to start businesses that would increase economic growth and employment opportunities in impoverished second and third world populations. Like the Gorky mission, this ministry also involved bringing qualified business people overseas for training conferences, as well as consulting for businesses and guest lectures at business schools and universities. Providing capital for new businesses opened opportunities for long term discipleship and a higher likelihood of sustainability.

Ziebell Associates' seminar program was extended for a second year. Every seminar leader brought in Bibles and Christian books written by forty-four different Christian authors. The total number it items carried into Russia was 2,018 Bibles and Christian books in the Russian language. In addition, there were 65 English language books and 51 audio sermons and 12 videos in English and Russian. Many of those items were given to the Gorky Baptist Church for their library and outreach ministry and for fund raising for building their new church. Slavic Gospel Association shipped directly to the church large quantities of Russian language Bibles, Children's Picture Bibles and Christian books from its shipping location in Germany.

For both years, all the American seminar leaders attended the worship services with the Gorky Baptist Church. It was for this reason I received the following letter from Pastor Vasily dated April 24, 1991:

Dear Donn G. Ziebell,

We seize every opportunity to extend to you our most sincere gratitude and our deepest respect for the strenuous efforts you take to reinforce Christian belief in our beloved but devoid of the Lord land!

Since God guided you to us in August 1990 very happy occasions began to happen: every month we had our brother from the USA to pray jointly with us.

Our brothers ' in Christ comings here show to all the people that Christians all over the world make up one body, the body of Christ, our Savior. By this way many people awakened for the Lord and joined our church. We thank you for this.

Some other people began to respect us more because they think, "Hay, these Americans who come here are intelligent individuals of good character. They are happy with God. Let us follow their path. We want to be like them."

The assistance which we received from you helped us raise funds to complete the construction of our new church building: to sum it up, the comings of our brothers from the USA helped us tremendously in the financial aspect and won a new flock for our church.

We are looking forward to seeing our American brothers and sharing the joy of a prayer with them in the future. We pray this come true.

Very truly yours, your brothers and sisters in Christ, members of the community of Evangelist Christian Baptists of the City of Nizhny-Novgorod.

Attached to the letter were three pages of 131 handwritten signatures by church members.

An Extraordinary Epilogue Ending

I must relate a most unusual occurrence that happened before any of the Ziebell Associates events took place in Nizhny Novgorod, Russia. It happened a month before my arrival in Russia to conduct the first seminar week mid-August, 1990. Pastor Vasily had a dream very early in July of 1990. God made a promise to him in a dream. Then during the July 22, 1990 worship service in Gorky Baptist Church, he told his dream to the congregation. His willingness to tell the congregation demonstrated his belief in having a true promise from God

Pastor Vasily Speaking to His congregation

Vasily dreamed he was walking on a path when he came upon a closed chest. He asked God what it was and he was told to open it. As Vasily looked in he asked, "What is it?" God said, "Gold." Then he continued to walk on the path and came to a second chest. The question and answer was the same. And it was the same with a third and fourth chest. When he came to the fifth chest on the path and looked in it, he asked God, "What is it?" This time God said, "It is Gold and I am sending it to you."

As you have read, I held the first seminar in the middle of August, 1990. I was the first American to show up at the church to worship with them and to give them Bibles and Christian literature. A different associate followed me in September, October and November to worship and bring Bibles and books. The fifth seminar leader, Pastor John Warton, arrived in February of 1991. He delivered more Bibles and books to the church and worshiped with the congregation.

Pastor Vasily revealed his dream to John Warton, the fifth American to come to the church, Before John left Russia to return home, Pastor Vasily gave John a gift to our church; a large Khokhloma platter with five matching bowls. Khokhloma is a unique Russian product of hand painted wooden items that include serving platters, bowls, utensils and the famous Matryoshka nesting dolls available on Amazon. Some household items of furniture are also included in the factory product line.

Vasily's gift contained four matching bowls with black lacquer inside of them to represent the first four chests on the path and the first four Americans to come to his church. The fifth bowl had gold lacquer inside it to represent the fifth chest and God making the promise to Pastor Vasily. John Warton was the fifth American to bring "gold" in the form of Bibles and Christian books, thus fulfilling the dream that enabled the congregation to build a new church.

The symbolism of the four black bowls and one gold lacquered bowl demonstrated God had fulfilled his promise to Vasily. It was wonderful to hear and know how God can and does communicate with his faithful believers. The first five American men were unaware at the time that they were participants in the fulfillment of God's promise to Vasily.

In 2001 Pastor Vasily Semyonov passed into presence of our God who made the promise of sending "gold" to him in a dream, and God's promise to Vasily was exceedingly fulfilled.

Khokhloma with Gold Lacquer inside the Bowl

About the Author

D onn Ziebell's pursuit in doctoral studies with The Union Institute University, Cincinnati, Ohio, intersected simultaneously with his receiving of the approvals from Moscow's Russian Ministry of Education and the KGB to present business seminars in Russia. Delivering his first in a series of lectures in August 1990, the seminar program proceeded with his sending a number of US instructors with specific disciplines into Russia to lecture on their business areas of expertise. Specific designated subjects for in-country societal observations by lecturers were reported within their trip reports. They provided valuable resource material for writing a cross-cultural experiential dissertation to complete his Ph.D. degree. His dissertation, "*A Model Combining Business and Evangelism for Mission Work in the Soviet Union during the Time of Perestroika,*" is in the libraries of thirty-one U.S. universities and seminaries.

Previously, his B.S in Metallurgical Engineering from the U. of Missouri, Rolla, and a MBA degree With Distinction from the U. of New Haven, West Haven, Connecticut, expedited his earlier career in manufacturing and consulting roles within Fortune 500 Corporations for thirty years. Then his executive management experience was effectively applied within Christian Mission organizations for an additional sixteen years before retiring. At the specific request of the Executive Director of one mission, Donn fulfilled the requirements through his home church to become a licensed minister in The Evangelical Free Church of America. He held this ministers license for a number of years while working as an executive, consecutively, in three U.S. mission organizations plus serving as a church elder.

His boyhood Midwest family-life values included art, letter writing, camping vacations and story-telling. He started oil painting during college semester breaks. His paintings create visual stories further expanded by their titles and can be viewed on YurArt.com. Years later he wrote a series of short stories about a fictional character that attracted a following within a community of people. They affirmed his writing as greatly entertaining and they eagerly anticipated reading the next story in the series. This response gave affirmation to his enjoyment of writing.

Donn G. Ziebell, Ph.D. authored three non-fiction published books of memoirs. Using a selection from his many letters written to a prisoner he covers a broad spectrum if interesting personal experiences: *My Letters to a Prisoner – I had not met*. His second book *Conceal Carry; Pause*, provides his inside findings about training as he learns about being an armed citizen for self-defense. It is a great book for anyone considering carrying a gun which is not that simple. Book three, *Gorky, Russia; First man in*, briefly covers his stops and restart corporate career; experience gained was later used in an executive position in a Christian mission. The reader follows him as the first American allowed into a Russian exile city closed to foreigners. While facilitating a week long business seminar to Russian industry leaders, three weeks in Nizhny Novgorod provided varied learning experiences all very unique and entertaining. Contact with the author can be made through his email address, but please use the title of one of his books for the email subject line so it is not deleted due to a select error: donnziebell@comcast.net

Made in the USA
Lexington, KY
29 April 2018